Cambridge Elements

Elements in Public and Nonprofit Administration
edited by
Andrew Whitford
University of Georgia
Robert Christensen
Brigham Young University

STANDING UP FOR NONPROFITS

Advocacy on Federal, Sector-wide Issues

Alan J. Abramson
George Mason University

Benjamin Soskis
Urban Institute

Shaftesbury Road, Cambridge CB2 8EA, United Kingdom

One Liberty Plaza, 20th Floor, New York, NY 10006, USA

477 Williamstown Road, Port Melbourne, VIC 3207, Australia

314–321, 3rd Floor, Plot 3, Splendor Forum, Jasola District Centre, New Delhi – 110025, India

103 Penang Road, #05–06/07, Visioncrest Commercial, Singapore 238467

Cambridge University Press is part of Cambridge University Press & Assessment, a department of the University of Cambridge.

We share the University's mission to contribute to society through the pursuit of education, learning and research at the highest international levels of excellence.

www.cambridge.org
Information on this title: www.cambridge.org/9781009475976

DOI: 10.1017/9781009401081

© Alan J. Abramson and Benjamin Soskis 2024

This publication is in copyright. Subject to statutory exception and to the provisions of relevant collective licensing agreements, with the exception of the Creative Commons version the link for which is provided below, no reproduction of any part may take place without the written permission of Cambridge University Press & Assessment.

An online version of this work is published at doi.org/10.1017/9781009401081 under a Creative Commons Open Access license CC-BY 4.0

When citing this work, please include a reference to the DOI 10.1017/9781009401081

First published 2024

A catalogue record for this publication is available from the British Library.

ISBN 978-1-009-47597-6 Hardback
ISBN 978-1-009-40109-8 Paperback
ISSN 2515-4303 (online)
ISSN 2515-429X (print)

Cambridge University Press & Assessment has no responsibility for the persistence or accuracy of URLs for external or third-party internet websites referred to in this publication and does not guarantee that any content on such websites is, or will remain, accurate or appropriate.

Standing Up for Nonprofits

Advocacy on Federal, Sector-wide Issues

Elements in Public and Nonprofit Administration

DOI: 10.1017/9781009401081
First published online: June 2024

Alan J. Abramson
George Mason University

Benjamin Soskis
Urban Institute

Author for correspondence: Alan J. Abramson, aabramso@gmu.edu

Abstract: This Element examines the recent history of nonprofit sector-wide advocacy at the federal level, focusing on work done by national nonprofit infrastructure organizations and national charities, to advocate on issues, such as tax incentives for charitable giving, that affect a broad range of nonprofits. The Element draws on interviews with thirty-nine national and state nonprofit leaders and federal policymakers as well as published papers and journalistic accounts. It finds that many policymakers are only weakly supportive of the nonprofit sector. In the end, this Element points to an uneasy, shifting balance in nonprofit sector advocacy between informal, decentralized, issue-based coalitions focused on short-term, if vital, legislative victories, on one hand, and the public good mandate embraced by some sector-wide advocates, which attends to longer time horizons and a broad conception of the defense of civil society, on the other. This title is also available as Open Access on Cambridge Core.

Keywords: nonprofit advocacy, nonprofit policy, philanthropy policy, nonprofit sector, philanthropy sector

© Alan J. Abramson and Benjamin Soskis 2024

ISBNs: 9781009475976 (HB), 9781009401098 (PB), 9781009401081 (OC)
ISSNs: 2515-4303 (online), 2515-429X (print)

Contents

1 Introduction   1

2 Major, Federal, Sector-Wide Advocacy Organizations   4

3 Sector-Wide Issues   10

4 Sector-Wide Advocacy Resources and Tactics   16

5 Effective Nonprofit Sector Advocacy: Grasstops Strategy   18

6 Two Conceptions of Sector-Wide Advocacy: Special versus Public Interest   20

7 Challenges: Cultivating Champions and Navigating Partisanship   23

8 The Fracturing of Advocacy Infrastructure and the Growth of Issue-Based Coalitions   24

9 Tax Cuts and Jobs Act: A Case Study   29

10 Post-TCJA Revisions and Reassessments   43

11 Sector-Wide Advocacy in Response to the COVID-19 Crisis   48

12 Sector-Wide Advocacy and Philanthropic Reform   52

13 State- and Local-Level Advocacy on Sector-Wide Issues   55

14 Recommendations for Enhancing Sector-Wide Advocacy   56

15 Conclusion   63

References   65

1 Introduction

From Alexis de Tocqueville's (1969) well-known chronicle of the United States in the early 1800s, *Democracy in America*, we know that associational, or nonprofit, activity, is a long-standing feature of American culture. And, with the nonprofit sector currently employing approximately 10 percent of the nation's private (i.e., nongovernmental) workforce, behind only "retail trade" and "accommodation and food services" and ahead of "manufacturing," this sector remains an important part of the nation's economic and social life today (Salamon and Newhouse, 2020). With the sector's importance and its general popularity with the public, it is not surprising that in recent decades sector leaders have managed several important public policy victories at the federal level (e.g., the enactment of the mandate that nonprofits paid with federal funds should receive at least some reimbursement for overhead expenses) and fended off a few serious attacks on sector interests (e.g., proposals to cap the deductions that can be itemized by wealthy taxpayers).[1]

However, at the same time that nonprofit leaders have achieved some advocacy successes, they have also been frustrated by their inability to advance sector interests even further, including in the face of the damage to sector interests sustained by the passage of the 2017 Tax Cuts and Jobs Act (TCJA) that is described in this Element.

Why has this important and generally popular nonprofit sector not done better in its public policy advocacy efforts? To address this puzzle, this Element examines the recent history and contemporary practice of federal-level, nonprofit sector-wide advocacy, defined as the work done by nonprofits, and especially national, nonprofit infrastructure organizations and national charities, to advocate on issues that apply to a broad cross section of the charitable (i.e., 501(c)(3)) portion of the nonprofit sector, spanning nonprofit health, education, human service, and other subsectors.[2] As discussed further in Section 3, among these federal, sector-wide issues that are of concern to nonprofit leaders are tax breaks for charitable donations and regulations concerning nonprofit lobbying and engagement in elections.

---

[1] On the sector's popularity, an Independent Sector (2021) report indicates that in 2021, 84 percent of survey respondents said they are confident in the ability of nonprofits to strengthen American society, and 57 percent of the public trusts nonprofits to do what is right. Trust in the nonprofit sector remains higher than in some other institutions in the United States, including government and the media, but has generally declined over the last decade as it has for many other institutions. See also various annual reports on the Edelman Trust Barometer (Edelman, various years). For another discussion of the nonprofit sector's recent policy record, see Abramson (2016).

[2] Nonprofit infrastructure organizations support other nonprofits by improving their effectiveness and representing them in the policymaking process. For more on nonprofit infrastructure organizations, see Abramson and McCarthy (2012).

Federal-level, nonprofit sector-wide advocacy is currently dominated by five, major, national, nonprofit infrastructure groups – the Council on Foundations (COF), Independent Sector, National Council of Nonprofits, Philanthropy Roundtable, and United Philanthropy Forum – and they sit at the center of this analysis (see Section 2 for short descriptions of the five organizations). So too do several of the major national charities, such as United Way Worldwide, Jewish Federations of North America, and the YMCA of the USA, whose policy staffers have also taken an active role in promoting policies related to charitable giving. Several ad hoc and long-standing coalitions, such as the Charitable Giving Coalition and Leadership 18, involving many of the organizations named above in this paragrpah, have been an additional important feature of the advocacy landscape.

The Element is based on telephone interviews, averaging about one hour in length, with thirty-nine individuals – twenty-one with current or former staff or consultants to national, nonprofit infrastructure organizations or other national charities, ten with current or former congressional staff, and eight with state-level advocates. One individual was interviewed three times, two individuals were interviewed twice, and on two occasions two individuals were interviewed together. We assigned interviewees to one of the two categories – nonprofit or congressional staff – based on their primary perspective during their interviews. Note that several interviewees have had significant experience in both nonprofit and congressional staff positions, and were difficult to place in only one of the two categories. Interviewees were promised anonymity to encourage their candor in discussing their own and their colleagues' advocacy activities, and so are not quoted by name in this Element. In addition to interviews, we drew on published papers from national infrastructure organizations and journalistic accounts of nonprofit sector-wide advocacy generally and of advocacy related specifically to the 2017 TCJA and congressional action in 2020 around COVID-19 relief and economic stimulus.

The Element largely covers new ground that is not addressed in the existing literature. This study takes a historical approach in contrast to many nonprofit research projects that employ social science methods.[3] Studies of nonprofit advocacy are increasing, but many analyses focus on advocacy by individual nonprofit organizations or on advocacy for subsector interests in fields such as healthcare, education, and the arts.[4] On nonprofit sector-wide advocacy, the work of historian Peter Dobkin Hall is relevant, especially his 1992 book, *Inventing the Nonprofit Sector*, but Hall's work does not cover the most recent

---

[3] Social science papers dominate the content of the nonprofit research field's major journal, *Nonprofit and Voluntary Sector Quarterly*.

[4] For a recent review of research on nonprofit advocacy, see Suarez (2020).

decades of sector-wide advocacy. Alan Abramson's 2016 article in *Nonprofit Policy Forum* describes the major obstacles to nonprofit sector-wide advocacy, but is a shorter treatment that does not contain the discussions of advocacy strategies and tactics and case study details that are included in this Element. A 2021 paper by Williams and Doan, also in *Nonprofit Policy Forum,* focuses largely on the evolution of one important advocacy organization, Independent Sector.

This Element also makes a significant contribution in its analysis of the friction between two models of nonprofit advocacy, one emphasizing nonprofits' public-interest orientation and the other highlighting nonprofits' attention to their own private, particular organizational interests. That is, one of the central tensions that defines the nonprofit sector in the United States is that it is organized around the promotion of the public good and yet relies on voluntary institutions with their own distinct organizational concerns.

This tension is especially evident in nonprofit sector-wide advocacy, the efforts of the nonprofit sector to advocate on issues that apply to a broad cross section of nonprofit organizations, spanning nonprofit subsectors. On the one hand, many nonprofit advocates regard their advocacy efforts as uniquely characterized by the attempt to promote the public interest. On the other hand, this advocacy can also be understood as no different from that of other trade associations promoting their own particular interests. The story of the continuing tension between the "public good" and "trade association" models of nonprofit advocacy is a central feature of this Element.

In focusing on issues that apply to all or almost all nonprofits, the Element does not address nonprofit subsector policy issues, such as those related exclusively to health, education, or arts nonprofits. Although it does not completely ignore work done at the state and local level or directed toward federal agencies, its concern is largely federal-level, nonprofit sector-wide advocacy targeting Congress within the last decade and a half.

The Element chronicles the development of the current nonprofit sector-wide advocacy landscape. It begins by introducing major, federal, sector-wide advocates, including the "Big Five" advocacy organizations, and noting the broad range of issues considered by nonprofit advocates to be sector-wide; it sketches out the current state of resources devoted to nonprofit sector-wide advocacy by the organizations most active in engaging those issues and describes the tactics and strategies advocates deem most effective, with a particular emphasis on developing and coordinating "grasstops" local champions of nonprofit sector-wide issues. It then considers the two, distinct conceptions of nonprofit sector-wide advocacy – the first which understands nonprofit sector advocates as constituting interest groups, similar to those representing the institutional interests of business-related industry groups, and the second which regards nonprofit sector advocates as engaged in a distinctive enterprise, based on the principle that, unlike other industries, nonprofits' primary interest is the public good.

Next, the Element discusses the challenges faced by nonprofit sector-wide advocates in cultivating champions and in navigating partisanship. It then chronicles one of the most significant developments in the recent history of nonprofit sector-wide advocacy: the fracturing of a centralized advocacy infrastructure and the growth of informal, issue-based coalitions, exemplified by the Charitable Giving Coalition. It then details two, short case studies in which many of these dynamics are exhibited: sector-wide advocacy during the TCJA, and advocacy in relation to congressional stimulus legislation in response to the coronavirus pandemic. Next, it briefly considers sector-wide advocacy in relation to campaigns for philanthropic reform. It ends with a discussion of recommendations for strengthening nonprofit sector-wide advocacy and brief reflections on what current dynamics suggest about the future of this advocacy.

2 Major, Federal, Sector-Wide Advocacy Organizations

Much of the advocacy on federal, nonprofit sector-wide policy issues discussed in this Element was conducted by five national nonprofit infrastructure organizations: Independent Sector, the National Council of Nonprofits, the Council on Foundations the Philanthropy Roundtable, and the United Philanthropy Forum. The following are short descriptions of these "Big Five" advocates, as some of our interviewees referred to them, along with some other coalitions and organizations that are important sector-wide advocates.

2.1 Independent Sector

Independent Sector (IS) was established in 1980 with the mission of serving as a "vital meeting ground" that brings together foundations and corporate giving programs, which might also belong to the COF, with other nonprofit organizations. Today, IS's membership totals approximately 465 grant makers and grant seekers, including the Ford Foundation, Bill and Melinda Gates Foundation, William and Flora Hewlett Foundation, YMCA of the USA, Boys & Girls Clubs of America, and United Way Worldwide, for example. Today, IS's strategic priorities include advancing the health of the nonprofit sector; building a community "to ensure all people thrive"; and, especially relevant for this Element, advocating on sector-wide, nonprofit public policy issues. The organization reported 2022 spending of $11.0 million to advance these goals. During most of the period covered in this Element, IS was led by Diana Aviv and Dan

Cardinali, with Akilah Watkins becoming IS's new president and CEO in January 2023.[5]

In response to new restrictions on foundations imposed by the 1969 Tax Reform Act, John D. Rockefeller III and other philanthropic leaders sought ways to bolster the foundation community and protect it from future policy attacks. To do so, these leaders supported the establishment in the mid-1970s of the Commission on Private Philanthropy and Public Needs (the Filer Commission), led by John Filer, CEO of the Aetna insurance company, which undertook a comprehensive assessment of the nonprofit sector. In its work, the Filer Commission supported the notion that foundations and the more popular, service-providing nonprofits from all subsectors were part of one nonprofit sector, a perspective that offered beleaguered foundations some of the cover and protection they sought (Abramson and McCarthy, 2012).

An important commission recommendation called for the establishment of a quasi-governmental body as "necessary for the growth, perhaps even the survival of the sector as an effective instrument of individual initiative and social progress" (Filer Commission report quoted in Abramson and McCarthy, 2012). When both government and philanthropic leaders balked at creating a new entity with official links to the government, a new private organization, Independent Sector, was formed through the merger of the National Council on Philanthropy and the Coalition of National Voluntary Organizations. The need to respond to critical public policy challenges posed by Reagan administration policies in the early 1980s and hostile hearings led by Senator Charles Grassley in the 2000s led to the strengthening of Independent Sector as an important advocate on sector-wide issues (Abramson and McCarthy, 2012).

Because of its membership and funding base and perhaps as a trade-off for becoming a strong voice on sector-wide issues, throughout much of its history Independent Sector has been seen as a voice especially of big, national non-profits and foundations and as working to defend the nonprofit sector as it already exists (Williams and Doan, 2021). According to this critique, Independent Sector has shortchanged local, reform-oriented, social justice organizations in much of its policy and other work.

2.2 National Council of Nonprofits

The National Council of Nonprofits (the National Council or NCN), formerly the National Council of Nonprofit Associations (NCNA), was established in 1989 as a "network of networks" that brings together the nation's state and regional nonprofit associations, which themselves are membership

---

[5] https://independentsector.org/

networks. Today, the National Council's network includes more than 50 state nonprofit associations and similar organizations representing 25,000 diverse nonprofits around the country. The National Council of Nonprofit's 2022 spending for its policy and other work totaled $2.2 million. In recent decades, the National Council has been led by Audrey Alvarado and, since 2008, by Tim Delaney.[6]

While Independent Sector has been seen as representing big nonprofits – and foundations – and especially focusing its work at the federal level, the National Council's constituency tilts toward small and medium-sized nonprofits in local communities, and the organization supports and undertakes advocacy and lobbying at the local, state, and federal levels to strengthen nonprofits.

The state nonprofit association movement gained momentum in the 1980s and 1990s with "devolution," the push by the Reagan administration and its allies to shift policy authority from the federal to the state level (Reid, 1999; Abramson and McCarthy, 2012). According to nonprofit expert Dennis Young, federal devolution initiatives seemed "to be the same kind of catalyst for organizing nonprofits at the state level in the 1990s that congressional attacks on foundations in the 1960s were for galvanizing collective action by the sector at the national level" (Young, 1999, cited in Abramson and McCarthy, 2012). As state nonprofit associations emerged, many of them became part of Independent Sector's network. Eventually, however, Independent Sector declined to be the hub for these organizations, and they subsequently formed their own association, then called the National Council of Nonprofit Associations, in 1989 (O'Connell, 1997). Since then NCNA/NCN and Independent Sector have often been collaborators – and sometimes rivals – in their work as sector advocates.

2.3 Council on Foundations

The COF (the Council) is a national membership association that is a voice for its foundation members. The Council, which took its current name in 1964 but dates its origins to the 1949 establishment of the National Committee on Foundations and Trusts for Community Welfare, now counts over 850 members, including a mix of private foundations, community foundations, corporate grant makers, and other philanthropies. The Council, which reported 2022 spending of $10.8 million, works to strengthen and encourage philanthropy, including through public policy advocacy, and increase public trust in foundations. In recent decades, the COF has been led by Dorothy Ridings, Steve

---

[6] https://www.councilofnonprofits.org/

Gunderson, Vikki Spruill, and, since 2019, Kathleen Enright, the Council's current president and CEO.[7]

Reflecting its membership, the Council has largely focused its policy work on matters affecting its grant-maker members, leaving Independent Sector and other entities to take the lead in sector-wide advocacy affecting the large number of charitable nonprofits that are not foundations. The Council and some other elements of the infrastructure for the foundation community were established and reinforced at least in part because of the perceived need by foundations for a strong advocate for foundations in a policy environment that often seemed hostile to these entities. Through the 1940s, 1950s, and 1960s, foundations were often under attack for one reason or another, including by Senator Joseph McCarthy and his anti-communist allies who charged that foundations were facilitating un-American activities and by Congressman Wright Patman who argued that wealthy foundations were accumulating too much economic and other power (Hall, 1992).

While foundations avoided unfavorable legislation through much of this period of hostility, the 1969 Tax Reform Act (TRA) established some new constraints on foundations, including requiring a minimum payout of foundation assets; establishing a 4 percent excise tax on net foundation investment income, which was reduced in later legislation; and setting penalties for self-dealing in which foundation board members, members of a foundation donor's family, or senior foundation staff benefit from transactions with the foundation (Council on Foundations, no date). As noted in Section 2.1, in response to the 1969 TRA the often-maligned foundation community sought to wrap itself more tightly with the more sympathetic other elements of the charitable nonprofit community. This interest in developing a coalition of foundations and other nonprofits helped lead to the formation of Independent Sector whose members include both grant-making foundations and grant-seeking nonprofits (Hall, 1992).

Like some other associations whose value for networking purposes has been weakened by advances in technology that provide alternatives to in-person conferences as methods for connecting, the Council has had a decline in membership over the last decade, falling from around 1,800 members in the early 2010s to 800–900 members in the early 2020s (Abramson and McCarthy, 2012). Some of the decline is due to the departure of COF members to other infrastructure groups, with, for example, some foundation affinity groups and regional associations of grantmakers

---

[7] https://cof.org/

affiliating with United Philanthropy Forum, community foundations joining CFLeads, and small foundations becoming members of Exponent Philanthropy.

2.4 Philanthropy Roundtable

The Philanthropy Roundtable (the Roundtable) was established as an independent entity in 1991 and is the voice of conservative foundations and donors, championing the cause of philanthropic freedom, the right of funders to give how, to whom, and to whatever causes they want to support. In 2022, the Roundtable registered $12.3 million in spending on policy and other initiatives funded through contributions from more than 600 member organizations and individuals. The organization's recent leaders have included long-time president and CEO Adam Meyerson, Elise Westhoff, and since 2023 Christie Herrera.[8]

The Roundtable began in the 1970s as an informal network of conservative grant makers under the auspices of the Institute for Educational Affairs and led by Leslie Lenkowsky.[9] The Roundtable gained membership in the 1980s when a group of conservative foundations left the COF rather than endorse the Council's new statement of "Principles and Practices of Effective Grantmaking," which encouraged foundations to see themselves as having responsibilities to the public and not just as entirely private institutions and included the suggestion that foundations diversify their staff and other decision-makers (Council on Foundations, 1980; Frumkin,1998; McDonald, 2021). As the Roundtable's first executive director put it, "What the council thought of as a more inclusive practice to grantmaking, the Roundtable's founders considered an intrusion on donors' independence" (Dennis, no date). Like other sector advocates, the Roundtable has been a collaborator on some efforts – and has been a sought-after partner especially when Republicans have controlled the White House and Congress – and an antagonist on others, with examples of both stances evident in the case study on the TCJA in Section 9.

2.5 United Philanthropy Forum

Somewhat similar to the birthing of the National Council of Nonprofits out of Independent Sector, the United Philanthropy Forum (the Forum or UPF), formerly the Forum of Regional Associations of Grantmakers, separated from

---

[8] https://www.philanthropyroundtable.org/
[9] https://www.philanthropyroundtable.org/history-of-the-philanthropy-roundtable/#:~:text=In%201987%2C%20IEA%20formally%20constituted,practice%20of%20effective%20charitable%20giving.

the COF in 1998 to become an independent organization. Like the National Council of Nonprofits, the Forum is a "network of networks," comprising regional associations of grant makers, foundation affinity groups, and other philanthropy-serving organizations, most of which themselves are membership associations. Today, the Forum comprises more than 90 member organizations, such as the Council of Michigan Foundations, Philanthropy Southeast, Grantmakers in Health, and Hispanics in Philanthropy, which, in turn, represent more than 7,000 philanthropic organizations. The Forum's 2022 expenditures of $4.4 million supported a variety of networking, knowledge-sharing, and advocacy activities. In recent decades, the Forum's leaders have included Alison Wiley, Ellen Barclay, Michael Litz, and, since 2016, David Biemesderfer.[10]

2.6 Other Major, Sector-Wide Advocates

While interviewees pointed to the Big Five as perhaps the most important sector-wide advocates, they named many other organizations – and coalitions of organizations – as also playing active roles on sector-wide issues in recent decades, especially around the TCJA and COVID as discussed in detail in this Element. As described in Section 8, the Charitable Giving Coalition emerged in 2009 because of dissatisfaction among some sector-wide advocates with Independent Sector's refusal to oppose the Obama administration's proposal to cap the charitable tax break for high-income taxpayers. The administration had developed the proposal to reduce the government's loss in revenue from the tax break in order to devote more funding for health-care reform. However, many nonprofits prioritized preserving the value of the charitable tax break over using potential savings for health-care reform, which they may have believed could be funded from other sources. The Charitable Giving Coalition, which now has almost 150 members, is narrowly focused on preserving – and expanding – the charitable deduction.[11]

Leadership 18 has been another important coalition active in advocating on sector-wide issues. This coalition now convenes twenty-two CEOs of the nation's largest human service organizations that "seek to share our knowledge and to pursue new approaches that expand our reach and our impact for the common good."[12] This group, and some of its individual members – including United Way Worldwide, YMCA of the USA, and Jewish Federations of North America – have been important advocates on many of the issues discussed in this Element, and their contributions are discussed in more detail in subsequent

---

[10] https://www.unitedphilforum.org/   [11] https://charitablegivingcoalition.org/members/
[12] https://leadership18.org/

sections of this Element. Other groups and coalitions have been involved more selectively on particular sector-wide issues that especially affect them, with, for example, religious groups engaged – on both sides – in the debate on the Johnson Amendment concerning the right of religious and other nonprofit organizations to engage in electoral activity (see Section 9).

3 Sector-Wide Issues

Nonprofit sector advocates interviewed for this Element, from the organizations described in Section 2 and others, all appreciated the distinction between subsector issues and sector-wide issues. There was an impressive range of issues that they cited as being of the latter type, with these issues falling generally into four broad categories: taxes and fees, regulation, government institutions and procedures, and government spending. Based on our interviews; a review of news articles and organizational documents, such as policy agendas and annual reports on policy activities; and other existing studies (see, e.g., Abramson, 2016), we identified the topics listed in Table 1 as major, nonprofit sector-wide, policy issues:

To be sure, however, only a handful of the issues listed in Table 1 were consistently cited as important by nearly all our interviewees. These standout issues include tax incentives for charitable giving; regulations regarding nonprofit advocacy, such as the Johnson Amendment which limits nonprofits' ability to engage in partisan electoral activity; and possible new rules regarding a required minimum payout from donor-advised funds (DAFs), which are funds that donors set up in 501(c)(3) charitable nonprofits, such as community foundations or charitable funds that have been established by Fidelity, Vanguard, and other financial firms. Donors can take a tax deduction when they add funds to a DAF and then advise on the distribution of the funds. For a donor, setting up a DAF is an alternative to creating the donor's own private foundation. One attraction of a DAF is that currently there is no minimum payment required for a DAF, whereas a private foundation must pay out 5 percent of its assets annually. Donor-advised funds have received increased attention, especially in recent years as the amount of funds held in DAFs has risen, leading some to want to establish a payout requirement to move more funding to nonprofits. These and other issues are discussed in Sections 3.1 and 3.2.

3.1 Federal Issues

3.1.1 Taxes

As noted at the start, the focus of this Element is federal, sector-wide issues, and the federal issue most often cited and which has received the most attention in

Table 1 Nonprofit, sector-wide policy issues.

Type of issue, governmental level, and policy issue

Taxes and fees
  Federal
    Tax deduction for charitable giving
    Estate tax
    Individual retirement account (IRA) tax rollover
    Unrelated business income tax (UBIT)
    Private foundation excise tax
    Incentives for volunteerism
  State and local
    Property tax
    Sales tax
    Payments and services-in-lieu-of-taxes (PILOTs and SILOTs)

Regulation
  Federal
    Nonprofit advocacy and election activity (e.g., Johnson Amendment)
    Nonprofit registration and reporting requirements
    Employee regulations (e.g., overtime rules, minimum wage)
  State and local
    Nonprofit registration and reporting
    Charitable fundraising
    Nonprofit advocacy

Government institutions and procedures
  Federal
    Contracting procedures: Application and reporting requirements, timely payments, overhead allowance
    Federal office on the nonprofit sector
    Internal Revenue Service (IRS) funding
    Electronic filing of IRS forms and public availability of this information
    Civic participation: Census, redistricting, voter registration, get-out-the-vote
  State and local
    Contracting procedures, allowable pay for nonprofit staff
    State offices on the nonprofit sector
    Funding for state charity officials
    Civic participation: Census, redistricting, voter registration, get-out-the-vote

Government spending
  Federal
    Spending on programs for which nonprofits are grantees, contractors, or otherwise funding beneficiaries (e.g., Paycheck Protection Program (PPP) assistance, postal subsidy)

Table 1 (cont.)

Support for nonprofit capacity building
Support for service/volunteer programs (e.g., AmeriCorps)
State and local
   Spending on programs for which nonprofits are grantees, contractors, or otherwise beneficiaries

---

recent years from advocates, and that gets the most attention in this Element, is charitable giving incentives in the tax code, and especially the promotion and defense of the charitable deduction. As noted in histories of the charitable deduction (Crandall-Hollick, 2020; Duquette, 2019), the charitable tax break was established in 1917 shortly after the enactment of the modern federal income tax in 1913. The sharp increase in tax rates in 1917 that was needed to help finance US involvement in World War I worried some who feared that wealthy philanthropists would have little money left over after paying their taxes to donate to charities, which would result in additional demands on a cash-strapped, wartime government. The hope was that a new charitable tax break, enacted along with the tax rate increase, would encourage the wealthy to maintain their giving.

The next major war, World War II, prompted the enactment of the Revenue Act of 1942 that added many middle-class Americans to the tax rolls for the first time to help pay for the war. However, the incentive for these new middle-class taxpayers to claim a charitable deduction to reduce their taxes was soon weakened by the Revenue Act of 1944. The 1944 act added the standard deduction to the tax code, in the process reducing the attractiveness of the charitable deduction for many middle-class taxpayers who could save more on their taxes by taking the standard deduction rather than by itemizing their charitable deductions.

The lack of a charitable tax break for many non-itemizing, middle- and low-income Americans was addressed by the Economic Recovery Act of 1981 which enabled non-itemizers to claim a deduction for their charitable giving. However, this non-itemizer tax break was phased out and not renewed in the Tax Reform Act of 1986.

Even more taxpayers became non-itemizers, with no access to the charitable tax break, as a result of the 2017 TCJA that significantly increased the standard deduction (see Section 9). As discussed further in Section 10, especially since the 2017 act, restoring a tax break for charitable giving by non-itemizers has been a major goal for nonprofit leaders.

To be sure, the salience of the charitable deduction issue to our interviewees does not mean it was necessarily the most important one to all sector-wide advocates, but it was the "one thing that people could agree and link arms on," as one advocate explained (though, as discussed in greater detail later in this Element, such unanimity was not absolute). Besides the charitable deduction, there are a host of other tax-related issues affecting charitable giving that sector-wide advocates are engaged with, including the individual retirement account (IRA) charitable rollover and the estate tax.

There are also tax-related issues that affect nonprofit practice, as opposed to charitable giving, such as the private foundation excise tax as well as issues related to nonprofit data disclosure, such as the recent successful campaign to mandate electronic filing of the Form 990 that nonprofits submit to the Internal Revenue Service (IRS) and the release of this information by the IRS in an open, machine-readable format.[13]

The unrelated business income tax (UBIT) is another tax-related, sector-wide issue that received some attention during the period covered in this Element. The unrelated business income tax requires a nonprofit to pay taxes on revenue that it receives as payment for providing goods or services that are unconnected to its charitable mission. For example, revenue earned by a museum store selling reproductions of art in its collection has been judged as "related" and exempt from taxation because it increases the public's understanding and appreciation of art. However, revenue received by the same museum store selling souvenirs of the city in which it is located has been found as unrelated to the museum's art-related mission and subject to UBIT. A nonprofit dedicated to preventing cruelty to animals that receives income from boarding and grooming services for pets of the general public must pay UBIT on this income because it is not related to its mission (Internal Revenue Service, 2021).

The UBIT was enacted in 1950 as concern grew about nonprofits engaging in inappropriate activities unrelated to their charitable mission and providing "unfair competition" to businesses that were engaged in similar activities but who also paid taxes (Arnsberger, Ludlum, Riley, & Stanton, 2008; Stone, 2005). A well-known example of nonprofit activity that helped lead to the enactment of UBIT was the owning and operating of the C. F. Mueller spaghetti and macaroni manufacturer by New York University. In advocating for the enactment of UBIT legislation, Representative John Dingell warned his colleagues that unless UBIT legislation was passed, "the macaroni monopoly will be in the hands of the universities ... Eventually all the noodles produced in this country

---

[13] https://www.aspeninstitute.org/blog-posts/new-law-brings-overdue-changes-to-nonprofit-tax-filings-form-990/

will be produced by corporations held or created by universities … " (Knoll, 2007). More recent policy activity related to UBIT is discussed in Section 9.

3.1.2 Regulation

Beyond tax issues, advocates also pay close attention to efforts to reform or regulate nonprofits, especially at the federal level, sometimes to encourage those efforts, other times to oppose them. The possible reform of donor-advised fund payout requirements, for instance, was frequently mentioned as an issue that advocates believed would occupy a considerable amount of time and energy in the near future. Government regulation of nonprofits' status as employers, including with regard to overtime rules, has also attracted attention.

Next to charitable giving incentives, regulations related to nonprofit advocacy were perhaps the second most frequently cited concern of sector-wide advocates. With this issue, the work of advocates involved not just advocating on those policies to lawmakers, but also educating the nonprofit sector on them. In recent years, this area has been dominated by the struggle to preserve the Johnson Amendment, which prohibits partisan, election-related activity by charitable nonprofits.

The amendment was introduced in 1954 by then Senator Lyndon Johnson who faced a political opponent whose campaign, during the McCarthy era of bitter attacks on suspected communists, was receiving significant funding from two major anti-communist nonprofit advocacy groups (Goldfeder and Terry, 2017). Enacted without congressional hearings or debate, the Johnson Amendment was originally motivated by a desire by Johnson and other politicians to keep nonprofits out of partisan politics. At the same time, it has also been supported by many nonprofit leaders who prefer to keep politics away from charitable nonprofits (Penna, 2018).

In his acceptance speech at the 2016 Republican National Convention, Donald Trump put repeal of the Johnson Amendment firmly on the political table, citing concern about the amendment's taking away the free speech rights of religious and other nonprofit leaders. Section 9 picks up the story of the Trump administration's effort to abolish the Johnson Amendment. According to some infrastructure organization leaders, for many locally based nonprofits, the preservation of the Johnson Amendment was the policy issue that activated the most interest in sector-wide advocacy, surpassing interest in charitable giving incentives.

3.1.3 Government Institutions and Procedures

Sector-wide advocates cited several other areas of work as important, including government contracting reform and efforts to establish a federal office on the nonprofit sector. Policies that would encourage volunteerism were also cited by a few sector-wide advocates, with several mentioning increased interest in the issue, though also noting it had not received nearly as much attention as policies related to charitable giving.

3.1.4 Government Spending

Nonprofit sector-wide advocates also made it clear that some of their sector-wide work involved promoting federal and state spending and budget policies that would benefit the nonprofit sector. And, they also sought to identify how nonprofits fit into and were affected by major pieces of legislation – such as the Affordable Care Act – and to flag concerns regarding unintended negative consequences of such legislation. In other words, sector-wide advocacy is approached not only as a matter of concern with specific policies but as a general form of attention and superintendence over government relations to the sector.

3.2 State and Local Issues

While federal nonprofit sector-wide issues are the focus of this Element, it is helpful to keep in mind that there are also many, critical, sector-wide matters that are decided at the state and local levels. State governments make their own decisions regarding issues that are also of concern at the federal level, including exemption from corporate income tax, tax breaks for charitable giving, nonprofit registration and reporting requirements, advocacy regulations, contracting procedures, and funding available for nonprofits. However, there are also some sector-wide issues that get particular attention at the state level, such as the duties required of nonprofit board members, nonprofit exemption from property and sales taxes, fundraising regulations, and allowable pay for nonprofit staff. Reflecting the significance of state regulations, it is state charity officials, often in state attorneys general offices, that have major responsibility for monitoring and enforcing laws and regulations affecting nonprofits even more than federal IRS staff.

A sector-wide issue in some localities is voluntary payments in lieu of taxes (PILOTs) by nonprofits. With municipalities under increasing fiscal pressure in recent decades, some cash-strapped cities, especially in the Northeast, have sought PILOTs from large, nonprofit hospitals and universities, which are often significant property owners that are not paying property taxes. The argument by these cities is that the nonprofits should reimburse the cities for the nonprofits' heavy use of city police, sanitation, and other services (Kenyon and Langley, 2010).

Not surprisingly, of course, there is significant variation in how many of these issues play out in different states and localities. While some recent studies have described and analyzed these variations, particularly around regulation of nonprofits (see, e.g., Lott et al., 2019; Lott et al., 2023; and Mitchell, 2023), there is a research gap that could usefully be filled by further examination of how nonprofit advocates seek to influence state and local sector-wide issues similar to the way this study is focused on nonprofit advocacy at the federal level.

4 Sector-Wide Advocacy Resources and Tactics

4.1 Advocacy Resources

The number of staff at nonprofit infrastructure organizations or national charities tasked with engaging in sector-wide advocacy as a primary responsibility has never been large, and it fell earlier in the last decade, as infrastructure organizations struggled with financial sustainability or underwent leadership changes.[14] Independent Sector's policy staff, for instance, shrank from seven to three full-time positions at the end of December 2016, just as tax reform, one of the most important issues to confront the sector, was preparing to heat up. However, it does seem as if in the last few years several infrastructure groups have experienced modest increases in policy staff with responsibility for sector-wide advocacy. It was only within the last few years, for instance, that United Philanthropy Forum could claim any full-time policy staff. Many of the leading national charities, such as United Way Worldwide, YMCA of the USA, and Jewish Federations of North America, as well as subsector advocacy organizations, such as the Council for Advancement and Support of Education, have designated policy staffers that work on issues related to charitable giving.

Some advocates pointedly mentioned the small proportion of organizational resources devoted to government relations and sector-wide advocacy as a leading explanation for nonprofit advocacy disappointments. But while advocates suggested that additional resources for advocacy would certainly be helpful, they also indicated that infrastructure organizations and national charities could do more with the resources they already have to advance effective sector-wide advocacy.

Advocates also made clear that their resources extended beyond paid staff. On the one hand, several advocates highlighted infrastructure organizations' increased use of consultants, often former congressional staffers, to take on lobbying responsibilities. To be sure, there was an undercurrent of criticism regarding this practice, because it prevented experience and relationships from developing internally within organizations and because there was some suspicion of consultants' mixed agendas, based on their assortment of clients. But

---

[14] For more on foundation funding of nonprofit infrastructure, see Bokoff et al. (2018).

more positively, sector advocates pointed out that infrastructure organizations and national charities with federated networks could also rely on their members' capacities and resources to undertake sector-wide advocacy. Since few of these locally based organizations have designated policy staff that focus on nonprofit sector-wide advocacy, their attention to sector-wide issues is variable. However, because of the large number of local organizations in federated networks, when engaged they can have a significant impact.

4.2 Advocacy Tactics

Nonprofit sector-wide advocates have adopted a wide range of approaches to their advocacy work. The most obvious of these is *direct lobbying*, whether targeting members of Congress and their staff, staff and leadership of executive branch offices and agencies, or state officials. But this lobbying often comes at the tail end of a much longer process of outreach, both on Capitol Hill and at the district level, to build relationships and educate lawmakers and their staff. This educative role is a key, if underappreciated, function of sector-wide advocacy, especially given the lack of familiarity of many members of Congress with the workings of nonprofits. Advocates frequently expressed surprise about the lack of sophistication of members of Congress and their staff when they discussed nonprofits. "I've sat in offices where people say, 'What do you mean people get paid in your sector? I thought it was the *voluntary* sector,'" one advocate recounted. Advocates also stressed that their engagement with lawmakers and regulators did not end once a law was passed; they needed to closely *follow policy implementation*, especially given the lack of familiarity with nonprofits among those they lobbied, although sector advocates also acknowledged that this dimension of their work had sometimes been neglected.

Sector advocates also directed much of their work back toward the nonprofit community, to *educate nonprofits* on major issues affecting the sector and to *cultivate community leaders to serve as advocates*. Sector-wide advocates appreciated that nonprofits, both large and small, had different attitudes with respect to their involvement in these sector-wide issues; some followed them closely while others delegated that responsibility entirely to infrastructure organizations or national advocacy organizations, relying on their attention and guidance to alert them when it was necessary to become active. As one advocate noted, "We're actually really good at getting people at a community level riled up."

Infrastructure organizations *trained member organizations in sector-wide advocacy methods*, providing them with materials, helping to craft messaging and to build advocacy capacity, and coordinating them in national campaigns.

They also had to push past two main challenges to grassroots activation: the lack of interest that some nonprofits had for sector-wide issues and confusion regarding the rules that might limit their participation in advocacy and lobbying.[15] Sector-wide advocates had to convince nonprofits of the importance of sector-wide issues and of nonprofits' right to advocate for them. But the education and guidance did not flow merely in one direction. Member organizations also reported back to national infrastructure organizations, helping to instruct them on the issues that were the highest priority to communities across the country and to hone their own messaging.

Finally, another advocacy role that some national infrastructure organizations have assumed is to *oversee the research landscape* as it relates to nonprofit policy change. This can involve commissioning new studies and disseminating new and existing data and research to help with sector-wide advocacy.

5 Effective Nonprofit Sector Advocacy: Grasstops Strategy

With striking and uncharacteristic unanimity, two related focus points emerged from discussions with both advocates and congressional staff regarding the most effective approach to nonprofit sector-wide advocacy. While abstract talk of civil society might impress some, more effective by far was demonstrating to policymakers the concrete good nonprofits do, especially how nonprofits benefit local communities. This includes the good that nonprofits do as employers, which has been a focus of nonprofit advocates of late, although there was some disagreement about how much it resonated on Capitol Hill.

The corollary to this, as it relates to charitable giving, was that political leaders care most about getting money into the coffers of these organizations. So, in debates about tax policy, advocates stressed the importance of shifting conversations from donor-centric preoccupations to discussions of how giving helps organizations on the ground, doing vital work within communities. The only caveat here was some uncertainty as to the significance Congress placed on charitable giving as a civic entitlement, that should be enjoyed by as many individuals as possible, with a value distinct from – if not unrelated to – the instrumental good it does in communities.

Given the consensus on the need to communicate to political leaders the good that nonprofits do in communities across the country and, in particular, in the districts or regions that politicians represent or have close relationships with, advocates also agreed on a particular tactic to accomplish this: a grasstops

---

[15] According to a recent report by the National Council of Nonprofits (2019), less than 3 percent of all 501(c)(3) nonprofits engage in lobbying of any kind, to say nothing of lobbying involving sector-wide issues.

strategy, in which leaders of local nonprofits, who might already have preexisting relationships with the politician or member of Congress in question and who might also already be contributing to their campaign, or might in the future, make the case on sector-wide issues. "When you've got local board members and respected leaders of the community who are well versed and tuned in to the right talking points ... that is, without a doubt, the single most important ingredient to success for nonprofits," explained one senior nonprofit advocate. Another claimed, "if it's a CEO of a local United Way, we have a pretty good shot of getting a member-level meeting in the district and a decent shot of getting a member-level meeting in Washington, DC." Community foundations were also cited as a useful ally in these communications, since their leaders often had close relations with lawmakers in their region. A few congressional staff also mentioned the sway that celebrities, like Bill Gates or the late Paul Newman, could hold if they took on issues related to nonprofits or charitable giving. In these assessments, the assumption was that sector-wide or national organizations could help facilitate these relationships and communications, but that their representatives and leaders would have much less sway with congressional members than local nonprofit leaders.

Given the consensus on the power of the grasstops strategy, it is somewhat surprising that several advocates acknowledged that until relatively recently, it had not received a great deal of investment from infrastructure organizations. Even during the peak of the lobbying campaign on the TCJA, one infrastructure staffer reported that the organization did not have adequate records of local nonprofit leaders who had existing relationships with members of Congress. Based on the resources that had previously been dedicated to this work, especially compared to the attention it receives from other industry interest groups, one advocate admitted that an observer would have to conclude that the nonprofit sector simply didn't prioritize government relations.

If that was true in the past, nearly all advocates believed it was no longer the case. They agreed that this sort of relationship mapping, involving the development and maintenance of comprehensive records of contacts, allies, and local champions in districts represented by key legislators, was an urgent task. It involves both the collection and collation of information by infrastructure organizations and advocacy coalitions to identify current local champions, but also the proactive recruitment of local nonprofit leaders to fill in gaps in relationships with key lawmakers.

In contrast to interviewees' emphasis on the importance of grasstops advocacy on sector-wide issues, there was little mention of grassroots activities involving the mobilization of ordinary citizens in sector-wide advocacy campaigns. Neither the Big Five nor other sector-wide advocacy organizations were especially equipped to do grassroots advocacy, and there were few signs of this kind of advocacy on the issues discussed in this Element, with advocacy around the Johnson Amendment being a bit of an exception with the engagement of some community members around the country beyond grasstops leaders (see Section 9). It may be that most sector-wide tax and regulatory issues are just not the kinds of issues that can ignite the interest of ordinary citizens or even of nonprofit clients who seem more likely to mobilize around particular government programs that touch them than broad, sector-wide issues whose impact on their lives is much less clear. While sector-wide advocates could undoubtedly benefit from increased grassroots advocacy, there are important challenges to expanding this approach, as described in Section 14.2. However, the importance of advocacy by **local** constituents to their elected representatives, whether the locals are grasstops or grassroots, is not in dispute.

6 Two Conceptions of Sector-Wide Advocacy: Special versus Public Interest

In surveying sector-wide advocacy over the last decade, two distinct conceptions of the sector *as a sector* emerge. In one, the nonprofit sector approaches policymakers as an interest group or trade association, much like a business association representing the banking, trucking, or hospitality industry. In this understanding, nonprofit sector-wide advocacy focuses on the promotion of the particular institutional interests of the sector's constituents, whether official members of sector-wide advocacy organizations or not.

In the alternative conception, sector-wide advocacy focuses not merely on institutional interests but on the good of civil society, broadly conceived. To the extent that it is oriented primarily, as opposed to indirectly, toward the public good, nonprofit sector-wide advocacy in this version is fundamentally different from and self-consciously contrasts itself with the advocacy associated with business-based sectors.[16]

The relationship between these two models has shaped how nonprofit leaders approach sector-wide advocacy. Some advocates have insisted that the sector's distinctiveness compared with conventional interest groups is its greatest asset, one which must be preserved at all costs. Adherents of this view think that it is precisely because many of those being lobbied believed nonprofits did not simply pursue their narrow institutional interests, but were stewards of the common good, that they would be receptive to sector-wide advocacy. And to

---

[16] For another discussion of this split between a trade association approach to sector-wide advocacy and an approach rooted in conceptions of the public good that emerged with the establishment of Independent Sector, see Williams and Doan (2021, pp. 16–18).

the extent that nonprofit sector-wide advocates modeled the tactics and messaging of trade association lobbyists, they threatened to undermine policymakers' faith in that distinctiveness which, they conceded, might also be simultaneously eroding for other reasons, such as high-profile scandals or nonprofits' embrace of business practices and for-profit modes of thinking. One nonprofit advocate even warned against infrastructure organizations placing ads in newspapers promoting the sector, since that move smacked too much of conventional interest-group lobbying. "It's always important to maintain your nonprofitness," the advocate instructed.

Other advocates framed the acknowledgment of nonprofit sector distinctiveness around a recognition of the sector's limits, as opposed to its strengths. They argued that because nonprofit sector advocates lacked the financial resources available to major trade associations that represented business and commercial industries – the US Chamber of Commerce and its subsidiaries spent nearly $95 million on lobbying in 2018, for instance – attempting to compete on these grounds places nonprofits at a natural disadvantage.[17]

Yet, while few advocates deny the potential utility of the idea of nonprofit distinctiveness, some take the opposite perspective and highlight the dangers of an overzealous commitment to it. It can, they point out, lead nonprofits to shy away from certain activities – such as lobbying on policies that affect their fundamental interests – deemed a violation of that identity. One advocate stressed that, even more significant than a differential of financial resources available to nonprofit and for-profit advocates, was a differential of "political will"; it was largely the unwillingness of nonprofit advocates to engage in politics that led to the lack of financial resources at their disposal.

Another critique of the emphasis on nonprofit distinctiveness was that it potentially blinded advocates to the ways in which they often did, in fact, operate much like traditional industry lobbyists. As one advocate commented, the funding model of infrastructure organizations, heavily reliant upon dues from members, encouraged those groups to justify the payments by delivering narrow, institutional "victories" for them. Furthermore, as several congressional staff pointed out, when advocates visited congressional offices with specific policies they wished to discuss – a universal charitable deduction or a revision of the private foundation excise tax, for instance – they were often assumed to be operating very much like lobbyists for other industries. By clinging too firmly to the pose of distinctiveness and institutional disinterestedness, advocates could become oblivious to the reality of how they were perceived, leaving them unprepared for reformist or regulatory attention. As one former

---

[17] https://www.opensecrets.org/federal-lobbying/clients/summary?cycle=2018&id=D000019798

congressional staffer noted, unlike some other sectors under congressional scrutiny, "[Nonprofit advocates] never really fully accepted that the message of 'we are special people, you cannot touch us' was going to fall flat."

Ultimately, most advocates believed that the choice between a trade association and a public interest mandate was not mutually exclusive and that it was possible to construct some amalgam of the two. Yet, at certain points, a stark contrast between them was posited, and advocates were compelled to make a choice. This was especially the case with respect to recent debates over proposals for the sector to establish a 501(c)(4) organization or a political action committee (PAC) to support sector-wide advocacy that could raise money and, according to the laws and regulations that govern these organizations, engage more directly in electoral politics and more heavily in lobbying activity.[18]

For some, if nonprofit sector advocates compete as one interest group among many, they do so at a considerable disadvantage because they lack the apparatus to direct financial resources to politicians favorable to their interests or to withhold financial support from those unfavorable. "Unless the sector develops the muscle to help or hurt candidates who back or oppose the things we want, then functioning as an interest group in that way is going to be minimally effective," one advocate explained. Supporters of establishing a 501(c)(4) nonprofit or PAC with the mission of advocating on sector-wide issues believe that there are enough wealthy individuals closely associated with nonprofits, as board members, for instance, to adequately fund a c4 or PAC to compete with those created by business associations. Some pointed to the 501(c)(4) recently set up by Americans for the Arts as an example.[19]

Not surprisingly, most of the advocates who believed nonprofit distinctiveness was a key asset considered developing a c4 or a PAC to be ultimately counter-productive, a squandering of the sector's reputational resources. "Charities are the good guys, so if we start acting like we're the muscle then we're just becoming another trade association," explained one advocacy leader. Another insisted that nonprofits had to remain "David" to other interest groups' "Goliath." Others pointed out the challenge of determining which candidates to back, especially with a broadly conceived understanding of the sector's mission to advance the public good, since there is no obvious, single, litmus test to apply. Should, for instance, a candidate who supports the universal charitable

---

[18] While 501(c)(3) nonprofits can not undertake a substantial amount of lobbying and are prohibited from engaging in partisan political activities, 501centralized advocacy nonprofits can do an unlimited amount of lobbying and involve themselves in partisan politics as long as this is not their primary purpose (Schadler, 2022).

[19] https://www.artsactionfund.org/what-we-stand

deduction, but opposes increased federal funding to the arts, or progressive taxation, receive a nonprofit PAC's support?

At this point, there seems to be little momentum behind the creation of a 501(c)(4) organization or PAC to conduct nonprofit sector-wide advocacy. But it remains a topic of discussion, a flashpoint for deeper debates over the nature of nonprofit sector identity.

7 Challenges: Cultivating Champions and Navigating Partisanship

Nonprofit sector-wide advocates largely believed that they could expect the general goodwill of political figures; no member of Congress would openly express hostility to nonprofits in general or deny the importance of civil society to the health of American society. But advocates frequently differentiated that vague and insubstantial support to a more vigorous championing of the sector. As one explained, "Everybody loves us, but nobody wants to marry us." Another commented, "When push comes to shove, we don't have people who are going to go to the mat for us." Ultimately, according to one former, senior congressional staffer, support "was plywood thin . . . I don't know that there is anybody that I would think of that [nonprofits and charitable giving] was the first thing that they cared about."

One of the main objectives of sector-wide advocates was to cultivate such figures in places of political power to encourage the creation of nonprofit *champions*. These were figures who would introduce bills promoting the interests of nonprofits and of charitable giving and convince others to do so as well. Champions were also willing to spend money on charities; otherwise, nonprofit advocates were compelled to pursue only revenue-neutral policies.

Advocates made clear that they hoped to recruit champions from either party; even as they tailored their arguments to Republicans – nonprofits as substitutes for government, or an emphasis on faith-based charities – or Democrats – nonprofits as instruments of equity – the nonprofit sector's nonpartisan and trans-ideological appeal was a central element of nonprofit sector-wide advocacy messaging.

Yet over the last decade, that idea of charity's nonpartisan appeal has had to confront the reality of surging partisanship and polarization. Several former congressional staffers mentioned suspicions that most leaders of nonprofits had Democratic leanings; one mentioned recently attending an annual meeting of one of the national infrastructure groups in which a speaker referred to "us" when speaking about Democrats potentially winning an upcoming election, a reflection of an unthinking assumption about the political allegiances of those in attendance.

Some sector advocates did acknowledge the dangers of the perception of being aligned with one party over the other, but most maintained that they continue to have strong relationships with both. Some even suggested that they were receiving more support from Republicans, dismissing the idea that Democrats were the sector's natural allies. They did, however, largely recognize partisanship as a force that increasingly complicated their advocacy work, introducing additional pressures on lawmakers and political officials that at times ran counter to the pressures advocates sought to apply.

8 The Fracturing of Advocacy Infrastructure and the Growth of Issue-Based Coalitions

One especially effective advocacy tactic that national infrastructure organizations have adopted in the past, and which was cited by several of the advocates consulted, was the position of being able to claim to represent broad swaths of civil society. When the sector spoke – or seemed to speak – in one voice through a lead advocate or organization united behind a particular policy position, Congress was more inclined to listen to what the sector had to say. When the sector spoke in a fractured voice, when there wasn't clear unanimity around policies or positions, sector advocates cautioned, policymakers were reluctant to throw their support behind any of them.

Yet, advocates also appreciated how difficult it was to sustain this consensus, especially given the vast range of organizations and institutions subsumed within the nonprofit sector and the priority the sector placed on pluralism. In the final decades of the twentieth century and in the early years of the twenty-first, various developments have amplified the sector's intrinsic fractiousness, unleashing centrifugal forces that fragmented a more centralized model of advocacy leadership exercised by the established infrastructure organizations into disparate issue-based coalitions and numerous subsector interest groups. This dynamic has amplified the perceived tension between the functions of sector-wide advocacy: defending the specific interests of nonprofit institutions and promoting the interests of civil society more generally.

Several of the advocates interviewed invoked the memory of Bob Smucker, Independent Sector's vice president for government relations during its first decades, in the 1980s and '90s, who expertly wrangled various member organizations into consensus, as an illustration of a since diminished model of strong, centralized, sector-wide advocacy. Yet the high-water mark for this model in recent decades likely occurred in the run-up to the Pension Protection Act (PPA) of 2006.[20] When Senators Chuck Grassley (R-Iowa) and Max Baucus (D-Montana) sought

---

[20] https://philanthropydaily.com/a-conversation-with-tax-policy-expert-dean-zerbe-part-2-of-2/

to craft legislation to reform the nonprofit sector, they worked closely with Diana Aviv, then president and CEO of Independent Sector. They requested Aviv, in part because of Aviv's own suggestion and consultation with Finance Committee staff, to form a panel of nonprofit leaders to recommend proposals, both with respect to legislation and sector self-regulation, "to assist our legislative efforts to improve oversight and governance of charitable organizations." They felt comfortable doing so because such a panel, under Aviv's leadership, could be credibly said to "represent" the sector. Aviv ultimately put together a twenty-four-member panel. The question of whether that representation led to results, in the package of reforms contained in the PPA, that were better for the sector than what would have been imposed on it without the panel, is an open one. So too is the question of how faithful that representation was; some organizations worried that their positions were not given adequate voice. In any case, the centralized model was always a somewhat unstable one (Wolverton, 2004).

The first major cracks in that model appeared around the proposal advanced by the Obama Administration in early 2009 to limit the tax break high-income taxpayers could receive for their itemized deductions, including the charitable deduction, at 28 percent (from 35 percent), and to use the savings to the Treasury to help create a $634-billion reserve fund to improve the health-care system (Perry, April 9, 2009d). Nonprofit leaders expressed a range of views on Obama's proposal. Some supported it out of a general desire to back the new Democratic president, and in response to pressure from the administration, and a belief that a limit on charitable deductions was a worthy price to pay for an improved health-care system, whose benefits would be enjoyed by many nonprofit organizations. In this view, health-care reform was in the public's interest, which was the interest nonprofits were ultimately tasked with promoting; to stand in the way of the proposal was to succumb to the impulses of a sectoral "interest group mentality." In contrast, other nonprofit leaders, including those from the United Way, the American Civil Liberties Union, and the heads of several fundraising professional associations, worried that the costs to charitable giving, and thus to nonprofit finances, would be too great (Perry and Preston, 2009).

Many of the major national charities that opposed the Obama proposal grew concerned that the leading infrastructure groups were not defending the charitable deduction vigorously enough. They worried, in a sense, that in endorsing a model of advocacy that promoted the public good, the infrastructure groups would neglect the promotion of a more proximate good, nonprofits' institutional interests. The COF had come out against the proposal, but Independent Sector had maintained a noncommittal position, with Aviv calling the proposal a Solomon's Choice and refusing to publicly oppose it (Perry, March 11, 2009a and March 27, 2009b).

It was out of frustration with that decision that the policy staff at several leading national charitable and fundraising organizations established the "Charitable Giving Coalition." The Coalition has no formal structure or designated staff; it relies on the advocacy resources of its member organizations, mostly large national charities. What it does have is a singular focus on the preservation of the charitable deduction. It has maintained that focus, helping to coordinate opposition to the capping of the charitable deduction as it reappeared in various legislative proposals over the next decade. While more research is needed to determine precisely how much credit the Coalition can take for scuttling the deduction limit, its members argue that it played a significant role in building opposition to the proposal on the Hill.

It is important to note that the genesis of the Charitable Giving Coalition was rooted in a *defensive* action; the defense of the charitable deduction could draw nonprofits into a shared advocacy campaign, without the emergence of a clear consensus around an affirmative or proactive program for supporting charitable giving. This defense of the deduction became one of the strongest bonding forces within sector-wide advocacy – though some claim its dominance has eclipsed other policies that were equally worthy of attention.

Initially, the Charitable Giving Coalition was formed as an alternative to IS, but after a number of years, as it became clear that policies promoting a cap on the charitable deduction would be a perennial challenge that the sector would need to regularly confront, IS joined the Giving Coalition and became an active member within it, as did the COF and the other national infrastructure groups.[21] Yet, according to several sector-wide advocates interviewed, the emergence of the Coalition did seem to reflect a downgrading in IS's prioritization of "interest group" sector-wide advocacy; it was still committed to that role, but not as its primary responsibility. Some traced this shift to Dan Cardinali replacing Aviv as president and CEO of IS in 2016; facing significant budget constraints, Cardinali reduced the number of policy staff soon after assuming the position (Koenig, 2016). This left an advocacy "void" or a "vacuum," these advocates explained, that the Charitable Giving Coalition, as well as other advocacy organizations, such as the National Council of Nonprofits, moved into, to take more leadership in direct, "interest group" advocacy around sector-wide issues.

This development represented a trade-off; interest-group sector-wide advocacy would lack the centralizing, unifying pole that a single, established infrastructure organization could provide and which could be key in developing

---

[21] https://charitablegivingcoalition.org/

a proactive reform agenda, or in managing the give-and-take between different preferred policies or interests within the sector – accepted under the directives of the common good. The weakening of centralizing forces within sector-wide advocacy could potentially contribute to policymakers' sense of the sector as fractured, which might in turn undermine the sector's influence. On the other hand, the weakening of those bonds freed up ad hoc and informal, issue-based coalitions to assume a greater degree of responsibility for sector-wide advocacy; they could likely do so with greater focus and agility for the particular interests and policies they sought to promote and defend than could an established infrastructure organization. Correspondingly, that dynamic could also free up established infrastructure organizations to assume novel forms of sector-wide leadership and advocacy that attended more directly to the relationship between civil society and the public good.

Over the next decade, the centrifugal forces continued to shape nonprofit sector-wide advocacy, as several other of these issue-based coalitions emerged, seeding a multipolar, advocacy landscape. Under the leadership of Adam Meyerson, the Philanthropy Roundtable began to engage more intensely with sector-wide advocacy, creating the Alliance for Charitable Reform (ACR) in 2005, in response to the push for nonprofit and charitable reform that led to the PPA.[22] The Roundtable and ACR are especially committed to the defense of donor prerogatives, privacy, and freedom from regulation and have developed strong connections to conservatives and Republican officials. More recently, Jeff Hammond, a former staffer in the office of Sen. Chuck Schumer (D-New York), began to represent private and especially community foundations on the Hill, assuming the position of a more traditional trade lobbyist, crafting a distinct advocacy position for community foundations. The rise of DAFs, which increasingly became a target for reformers and which provide significant funding for many community foundations, helped to precipitate this turn to trade association representation, reflecting concerns about the vulnerability of institutional interests which called out for active, targeted defending.

In the wake of the conflict over Obama's proposal to cap the charitable deduction, Leadership 18, which had been established earlier in the decade as an executive learning community made up of the head of United Way and the CEOs of many of the national social service nonprofits it funded, decided to take on an increased advocacy role on sector-wide issues as well.[23] Much like the Charitable Giving Coalition, with which it shared several key member organizations, Leadership 18 CEOs' ultimate turn to public advocacy stemmed from

---

[22] https://www.philanthropyroundtable.org/tag/alliance-for-charitable-reform/
[23] http://leadership18.org/about

a belief that their institutional interests were not being adequately championed by the existing infrastructure organizations. As its name attests, the group initially had eighteen members; it now has several more. The CEO of United Way Worldwide serves as its standing vice chair with the chair rotating among the other members.

A brief lull in major legislative action involving charitable giving after the initial clash over Obama's proposal obscured the full significance of the fracturing of sector-wide advocacy. But as legislative action picked back up – especially with the 2014 tax reform draft bill proposed by Representative David Camp (R-Michigan), which contained several provisions related to nonprofits and charitable giving – the new advocacy paradigm, dominated by informal, single-issue coalitions and the pursuit of particularistic interests, began to emerge more powerfully. Its benefits and flaws could be more clearly identified. Defenders saw it as consistent with the pluralism and diversity that was the strength of the sector. Given that reality, efforts to maintain too tight a hold through centralizing institutions will always be volatile, and consensus will always be difficult to sustain. Some organizations rely on charitable donations, others on government contracts, while others place more value on encouraging volunteering. Ad hoc, informal coalitions, operating outside the bounds of the established infrastructure organizations and built around particular issues, would attract and make the most effective use of those organizations for whom the issues were critical, allowing others to participate more variably – or not at all.

But some sector-wide advocates did acknowledge that such a structure came with a cost. A more fragmented model of advocacy could potentially erode a shared sense of sector-wide identity that was an important sector-wide asset and that fed some of the narratives behind key messaging. Even if issue-based coalitions were effective in defensive campaigns, beating back reforms that might damage certain institutional interests, how effective were they in crafting a "unifying narrative," one advocate asked, about the centrality of civil society in American life? They could tell many little stories well, but perhaps not one convincing, big story. Several congressional staff interviewed noted this danger, warning that the nonprofit sector had gained a reputation for disunity, which undermined its clout. Could more centrifugal forces be counterbalanced by centripetal ones, rooted in the more established infrastructure organizations, that considered the health and well-being of civil society in its broader configurations?

Further, it's worth asking the extent to which these more informal coalitions should be considered sector *infrastructure*. Would investments in them – of time and attention, if not necessarily of financial resources – result in a durable, long-term presence?

9 Tax Cuts and Jobs Act: A Case Study

Nearly all the dynamics that nonprofit advocates and congressional staff identified as key to understanding the development of sector-wide advocacy appeared in vivid relief during the lobbying and advocacy around the passage of the TCJA. Congress passed and President Trump signed the TCJA in December 2017. It was the largest rewrite of the United States tax code in over thirty years and included broad changes to the individual and corporate tax rules, most significantly a permanent reduction of the corporate tax rate. It also contains several provisions with significant impact on nonprofits and charitable giving. It was, not surprisingly, the object of intense lobbying by the business sector and specific subsectors of it – combined, the Chamber of Commerce, the Business Roundtable, and the National Association of Realtors spent more than $56 million on lobbying in the final quarter of 2017 – as well as by nonprofit advocacy organizations (Vogel and Tankersley, 2017; Gale et al., 2018; Brody, 2018).

Generally speaking, business lobbyists considered the TCJA a victory. This should not be especially surprising; the Center for Public Integrity identified sixty-three "major changes to the business tax code" in the bill, the vast majority favorable to business interests (Cary and Holmes, 2019). It represented a vindication in many respects of the vast apparatus of business-sector lobbying. But for many nonprofit advocates, it represented a significant disappointment and a sign of the sector's lack of clout. One former sector-wide advocate summed up the results of the sector's lobbying for the bill as "an unquestionable loss." Another admitted the nonprofit sector "got crushed." More specifically, looking back on the TCJA lobbying melee, some sector-wide advocates identified evidence of both the benefits and drawbacks of the sector's more fragmented, less cohesive model of advocacy. In this respect, the experience provided an education that would help set the sector up for more success during the COVID-19 crisis.

But there are two reasons why the TCJA offers an imperfect case study to gauge the effectiveness of nonprofit sector-wide advocacy. First, nearly all those interviewed for this Element remarked on what they believed to be the inevitability of the bill's passage and the intractability of several of its provisions that would likely have the most negative impact on the nonprofit sector. "When a bill is being written by just a few people and there's really nobody that can stop it, I don't want to beat myself up too much" for its passage, commented one advocate. "The Republicans were going to pass tax reform and anyone who got in their way was going to be steamrolled," another remarked. "And there wasn't a damn thing any of us could do."

Second, a large part of the damage the TCJA did to charitable giving, and the reason for much of the advocacy community's sense of demoralization, was *indirect*, through the near doubling of the standard deduction; the charitable sector, as one former congressional staffer explained, took on "unintended collateral damage" from that policy shift. "We have spent an enormous amount of time up on the Hill, and we get back the talking point, 'Oh, don't worry – we'll preserve the charitable deduction.' That makes it seem like many lawmakers don't understand, themselves, what the ramifications of this legislation are," Steven Taylor, senior vice president at United Way Worldwide, explained to the *Washington Post* in October 2017 (Johnson, 2017).[24]

For Taylor and other advocates, the persistence of this misunderstanding was the source of great frustration, and it offered little consolation to the nonprofits who would actually suffer the consequences of that collateral damage in reduced donations. But advocates did differentiate between policy setbacks that are the product of active legislative hostility and those that are the result of unintended consequences and the sector's lack of clout to prevent or compensate for them. While it was true that the "unquestionable loss" for the nonprofit sector that occurred in TCJA should compel some reassessment of strategy and messaging, they argued, the sort of panic that might be triggered after a failed targeted legislative campaign was not appropriate in this case.

The TCJA contained a number of provisions that, directly or indirectly, had a significant impact on nonprofits.[25] Most significantly it nearly doubled the standard deduction to $12,000 for individual filers and $24,000 for joint filers, and limited taxpayers' ability to deduct state, local, and property taxes. These changes decreased the incentives for taxpayers to itemize and therefore take the charitable deduction, which in turn weakened the incentives the tax code offers for charitable giving, which many analysts predicted would lead to a decrease in total giving, by some $13 billion, according to the most commonly cited study at the time.[26] A reduction in the top marginal income tax rates and a weakening of the estate tax also reduced the tax-related incentives to give. The bill did increase the adjusted gross income (AGI) limits on cash contributions to

---

[24] It's worth asking how much of a calculated pose by policymakers this seeming misunderstanding about the potential damage to charitable giving of increasing the standard deduction actually was. One advocate conceded that the fact that there was an increase in the AGI limitations for cash contributions to public charities in early drafts of the House bill suggests that Republicans were prepared relatively early for the criticism that charitable giving would likely be hurt by provisions within tax reform and wanted to offer some compensatory policies in response (see https://independentsector.org/blog/so-whats-in-the-house-tax-reform-bill/).
[25] https://independentsector.org/wp-content/uploads/2018/01/2017-final-tax-bill-summary.pdf
[26] https://independentsector.org/resource/tax-policy-and-charitable-giving/

charities from 50 percent to 60 percent, which analysts predicted would provide a modest boost to giving.

There were a number of provisions in the TCJA that reflect Congress's inclination to look to nonprofit institutions as revenue raisers, which they turned to in an effort to offset the enormous costs of other parts of the bill. The bill "impose[d] a 21 percent excise tax for individual compensation (cash and benefits, except retirement and health) in excess of $1 million for any one of the five highest compensated employees at charities." It imposed a 1.4 percent excise on the net investment income of the endowments of colleges and universities above a certain threshold of endowment size in proportion to the number of full-time students enrolled. Although not strictly a sector-wide issue, many sector-wide advocates tracked this provision closely because they feared it would set a precedent for using nonprofit endowments more generally as taxable sources of revenue (Wong and Fattal, 2017). Finally, it also modified the way that the UBIT is calculated, which sector advocates believed would likely result in tax increases for some nonprofits, and also imposed on nonprofits, including houses of worship, new tax liabilities on "qualified transportation benefits," such as parking.

Yet, it's also important to note what the TCJA did not include: two provisions whose absence should shape an assessment of nonprofit sector-wide advocacy. First, it did not include the repeal of the Johnson Amendment, the 1954 provision which prohibits religious institutions and 501(c)(3) nonprofits from supporting political candidates. President Trump had championed repeal – vowing to "totally destroy" the amendment earlier in the year – and repeal had been included in the version of the tax bill passed by the House in November 2017. But it was not included in the Senate's version, nor in the version that Trump ultimately signed into law. Protecting the Johnson Amendment was the object of a fierce lobbying campaign by a broad coalition of organizations (discussed below in this section), including several of the leading national nonprofit infrastructure groups, and the success of this effort tempered the disappointment of many sector advocates. But that disappointment was intense, largely because of another provision the TCJA did not include: any version of an above-the-line or universal charitable deduction, available to all taxpayers and not just to itemizers.[27] This was the primary focus

---

[27] "Above-the-line" deductions are adjustments to gross income that can generally be made by taxpayers whether they itemize their deductions or use the standard deduction. "Below-the-line" deductions to income are only available to the 10 percent of taxpayers who itemize their deductions and do not take advantage of the standard deduction. During the coronavirus pandemic, non-itemizers were able to deduct a capped amount of their charitable contributions. However, this privilege has expired, and currently, the charitable deduction is a below-the-line

of sector-wide advocacy during TCJA deliberations, and to the extent that advocates considered their work a "resounding defeat," as one termed it, it was due to their failure to secure its inclusion (Long, 2017).

Though the speed with which the TCJA worked its way through Congress took some advocates by surprise, most of the national infrastructure groups had been preparing for some version of tax reform for at least a year, hoping that it could provide an opportunity for boosting charitable incentives. In the spring of 2017, Independent Sector released the results of a poll showing broad support for a universal charitable deduction, and launched a campaign, Giving100, to promote the expansion of the charitable deduction, timed for the centennial of the deduction's creation in 1917.[28]

In December 2016, in an effort to educate and galvanize the sector on the potential for upcoming congressional battles, IS also commissioned research from the Lilly Family School of Philanthropy at Indiana University on the likely effects of tax reform on charitable giving, which was released in May 2017.[29] The research was meant to alert the sector to the fact that a defensive posture of preserving the deduction would not be adequate, and that some proactive policy with respect to charitable tax incentives would be necessary to compensate for the likely damage caused by tax reform.

At the same time, initial contacts with congressional offices brought back reassurances that the charitable deduction was safe. Because Congress was entirely in Republican hands, the ACR, with strong ties to some key Republican leaders, including Vice President Pence, took an especially prominent role in these early forays. The ACR's representatives gained heightened credibility in internal sector deliberations; they positioned themselves, as one advocate described it, as "Republican whisperers." In July 2017, as the White House announced that the administration would not pursue a border adjustment tax, under which goods would be taxed depending on where they are consumed rather than where they are produced, and the likely contours of tax reform became clearer, conservative-leaning nonprofit leaders, including the president of the Philanthropy Roundtable, met with Pence and congressional Republicans at the Eisenhower Executive Office Building, in a convening organized by ACR, to discuss the status of charitable giving in tax reform (Daniels and O'Neil, July 13, 2017b). Buoyed by the meeting, ACR lobbyists began to

---

deduction only available to itemizers. The universal charitable deduction would be an above-the-line deduction for non-itemizers so that they could also receive tax relief for their contributions.

[28] https://independentsector.org/blog/national-poll-finds-that-americans-strongly-support-expanding-charitable-deduction/; https://independentsector.org/blog/independent-sector-launches-awareness-campaign-to-expand-the-charitable-deduction/;

[29] https://independentsector.org/blog/new-research-shows-impact-of-tax-proposals/

reach out to congressional leaders about the possibility of supporting a universal charitable deduction, getting some initially promising responses. At the same time, Leadership 18, which had been applying more discreet behind-the-scenes pressure, began to issue public statements in support of a universal charitable deduction.[30]

As deliberations around tax reform began to heat up on the Hill, and as an increase to the standard deduction emerged as a key plank within it, the Charitable Giving Coalition took the lead as the primary entity to craft a sector-wide advocacy response, with national infrastructure organizations like IS and the COF participating alongside national charities (Davis & Rappaport, September 27, 2017; Swan, September 26, 2017). As the tax reform bill moved through Congress, and as advocacy pressures intensified, the Giving Coalition began to swell with new organizations, with some long-standing members complaining that it ultimately became unwieldy. Somewhat paradoxically, the Charitable Giving Coalition began to struggle with pressures similar to those experienced by the more established infrastructure organizations, as member organizations pushed the coalition to take up particular policies beyond charitable giving incentives and the coalition had to balance inclusion with focus. Independent Sector, for instance, urged the coalition to address the Johnson Amendment as well, but the nonprofits that dominated the coalition – particularly United Way Worldwide, the YMCA, and Jewish Federations – refused to do so.

By September 2017, as more details about the likely shape of tax reform emerged, sector-wide advocates undertook a vigorous lobbying campaign. They met frequently with members of Congress, with particular attention directed to the tax-writing committees, Senate Finance and House Ways and Means, securing meetings with the chairs of those committees. National infrastructure organizations reached out to their members, encouraging them to get in contact with their representatives to urge them to protect charitable giving and to promote the interests of nonprofits, with the National Council of Nonprofits especially active on this front.

Yet advocates faced a predicament with respect to the most problematic provision in the bill for charitable giving, the near doubling of the standard deduction. That provision represented a pillar of Republican efforts to simplify the tax code and to broaden the base of those receiving a lighter tax burden. Sector-wide advocates found themselves in a precarious position. To the extent they were perceived as opposing a significant increase to the standard deduction, they faced enormous blowback. "It was received

---

[30] http://leadership18.org/1257-2

terribly," noted a former congressional staffer. "It was viewed as selfish." It could be regarded, in a sense, as confirmation that the charitable sector had embraced the status of a trade association that places its own interests above the public good and was no different than the home-builders and realtors opposing revisions to deductions that would negatively affect their industries as well.

So, instead of directly opposing the increase to the standard deduction and on top of not initially opposing the tax bill more generally, sector-wide advocates largely settled on a strategy of accepting that increase but promoting an expansion of the charitable deduction as a way of compensating for it. That case relied heavily on research on the likely effects of the provisions in the tax reform bill on charitable giving by Indiana University, the Urban-Brookings Tax Policy Center, and the Joint Committee on Taxation. It required convincing somewhat uncharacteristically skeptical Republicans of the power that tax incentives had to shape individuals' charitable behavior. It's likely that no previous campaign by nonprofit sector-wide advocates was armed with as rich a cache of research, the product of a significant investment in studies by funders over the previous years.

Advocates appreciated that the data and research worked best when allied with key narratives and value-based arguments. The United Way, for instance, impressed policymakers that the declines in charitable giving that would be produced by the tax bill would likely fall heaviest on traditional charities like social service providers that lawmakers seemed to care the most about. As one advocate explained, "I love data. I'm also realistic to know that most legislators, most politicians and staff are impervious to data. What they are not impervious to is a call to the local talk radio host from the head of the food bank explaining how their donations are down. They are highly, highly reactive to certain key players back home saying, 'gosh, you voted for a law that reduced the total amount of dollars going to our homeless shelter.'"

But while sector-wide advocates generally agreed on this broad approach, they had more difficulty rallying around a specific policy response to it. The strongest consensus formed around some version of a universal charitable deduction (UCD), but without settling on its precise contours – whether a "clean" version, or one with a cap or a floor. In a foreshadowing of this difficulty, a 2011 effort sponsored by IS to discuss the promotion of a non-itemizer deduction had disbanded because of a failure to reach any consensus. The national charity leaders of the Charitable Giving Coalition pushed hardest for members to rally around a "clean" version, in part because they recognized that putting the sector's muscle behind a cap or a floor would mean alienating some advocates steadfastly against one or the other policy.

But when it became clear that, because of the large costs to the federal Treasury and the administrative burdens for tax authorities associated with a clean version, it had little political momentum on the Hill, sector advocates were unable to coalesce around another option. Some continued to hold out for the "clean" version, while others gravitated toward a UCD with a cap. In early October 2017, Rep. Mark Walker, a Republican from North Carolina, introduced a bill with a UCD with a $2,100 cap for individuals and $4,200 for married couples; in mid-November, Sen. James Lankford (R-Oklahoma) introduced a Senate version. Some advocates urged the coalition to fully back Walker's bill, but no consensus was reached.

The heads of IS, the COF, and the National Council of Nonprofits came out strongly against the House bill, which included the increase to the standard deduction without adding a UCD, and also included the repeal of the Johnson Amendment, publishing an ad in Politico warning that the House and Senate bills "threatened to undermine our nation's tradition of giving" and urging the House to vote against it.[31] When the bill passed on a largely party-line vote in mid-November, advocates shifted attention to the Senate, where they had received a more favorable reception from the Finance Committee.[32] But they ultimately had little success there either, as the Senate bill, which passed in early December, also lacked a UCD but did not include repeal of the Johnson Amendment. As the final version of the TCJA inched toward passage, sector-wide advocates debated whether, and when, to formally oppose it. In the end, just days before the TCJA passed, the COF, Independent Sector, and the National Council of Nonprofits issued a statement publicly opposing the bill, calling on Congress to "scrap this bill and start over."[33]

Of course, there were other provisions within the TCJA with impacts on the nonprofit sector besides those relating to tax deductions, and sector-wide advocates joined or formed coalitions to target several of them. Two leading examples are cited in the discussion that follows.

Estate Tax. The National Committee for Responsive Philanthropy led a group of largely progressive organizations, ultimately joined by IS, in publicly opposing revisions to the estate tax that would reduce it, and thereby reduce incentives to charitable giving.[34] Many sector-wide advocates chose to sit on the sidelines on the issue, believing there was little chance of success and wanting to keep

---

[31] https://independentsector.org/blog/infrastructure-organizations-unite-against-house-tax-reform-bill/
[32] https://clerk.house.gov/evs/2017/roll637.xml
[33] https://independentsector.org/blog/nonprofits-and-foundations-stand-united-in-opposition-to-the-tax-bill/
[34] https://independentsector.org/blog/independent-sector-statement-on-the-house-tax-reform-bill/

their "powder dry." The campaign ultimately failed, with the tax bill significantly increasing the exemption for the estate tax, although it did not repeal the estate tax, which was a modest victory (Daniels, 2017).

Johnson Amendment. There was some disagreement as to how large a priority to make opposing the repeal of the Johnson Amendment among sector-wide advocates. But the issue-based coalition model meant that those disagreements did not undermine the advocacy campaign, because those most dedicated to the issue could work together outside the bounds of a formal infrastructure organization or network.

Among the infrastructure groups, IS, the COF, and the National Council of Nonprofits took the lead in opposing repeal; some state-based or regional associations also took strong public stands.[35] Like other organizations opposing repeal, these groups argued that it would lead to a flood of political funding into nonprofits as well as pressure to engage in politics which could warp nonprofits' missions. The National Council of Nonprofits used its state- and local-based networks to connect more than 5,600 nonprofits, including churches and national charities like the American Red Cross that sought to preserve the amendment, to lawmakers who opposed repeal.[36] Independent Sector, the Council, and the National Council of Nonprofits took out an ad in *Roll Call* "to urge lawmakers to keep changes to the Johnson Amendment out of the final tax reform legislation negotiations."[37] IS also commissioned and publicized a poll that showed broad support for the amendment, even from Trump supporters. IS, the Council, and NCN joined a much broader coalition of organizations opposed to repeal, including many progressive and mainline religious organizations, as well as secular ones and organizations concerned about money in politics. Americans United for Separation of Church and State, for instance, brought together 4,300 faith leaders to offer support for preserving the amendment, and more than 10,000 of the organization's volunteer activists urged Congress to do so through emails, phone calls, or petitions (Vogel & Goodstein, 2017; Wilson, 2017).

This was the broadest-based coalition in which nonprofit sector-wide advocates engaged, and because of that breadth, it is difficult to determine how much credit they should receive for beating back repeal. They did play a significant role in the maneuver that had a large hand in ultimately scuttling the repeal: the decision by the Senate parliamentarian that the repeal of the amendment

---

[35] https://nonprofitquarterly.org/losing-johnson-amendment-destroy-unique-political-role-nonprofits/
[36] https://www.councilofnonprofits.org/sites/default/files/articles/community-letter-in-support-of-nonpartisanship-5-12-update.pdf
[37] https://independentsector.org/blog/drawing-clearer-lines-as-tax-reform-moves-forward/

violated the Byrd Rule, "which limits reconciliation provisions to those affecting revenue, spending, or deficit reduction," and which led the amendment to be stripped from the Senate bill. The National Council of Nonprofits gave last-minute research support and guidance to the parliamentarian to help make that determination (*Nonprofit Times*, 2017).

Opponents of repeal faced off against an impressive coalition of organizations, mostly allied with evangelical churches, in support, who could claim key congressional allies, including several, like Sen. Lankford and Rep. Walker, who were also champions of a universal charitable deduction. It is notable then, that in overall assessments of nonprofit sector-wide advocacy in the TCJA, the success in defending the Johnson Amendment is often overshadowed by the failure to win a UCD. The relationship between those two campaigns does raise intriguing questions about their divergent fates. Why did the sector succeed in one and not the other? The most obvious explanations are that a UCD's cost increased the level of the "ask" and that defensive lobbying is almost always easier than proactive lobbying. But it is also possible that the broad-based nature of the coalition defending the Johnson Amendment, which mobilized communities from across the country and from nearly every congressional district, provides a model of grassroots and grasstops mobilization that nonprofit sector-wide advocates must match for other priority issues to achieve sufficient legislative clout (Dias, 2017).

9.1 Challenges to Sector-Wide Advocacy during TCJA Negotiations

9.1.1 Republican Legislative Steamroller

As mentioned earlier, the speed with which the tax reform bill moved through Congress, and the ways in which Republicans rallied around its passage after their failure to dismantle President Obama's health-care reform earlier in the year, did not give nonprofit advocates time to mount a sustained campaign to educate policymakers on the benefits of a universal charitable deduction or to cultivate champions. "There was no effective advocacy because there was no time for it," one advocate explained. In fact, neither the House Ways and Means nor the Senate Finance committees scheduled hearings that allowed nonprofits to make their case on tax reform (Daniels and O'Neil, September 27, 2017a).

This was by design. Congress sought to expedite the passage of the TCJA by limiting the opportunities for lobbyists and interest groups to sink their teeth into it. Lawmakers accomplished this by drafting the bill with a very small group of legislators in order to decrease the risk of leaks from other members or their staff. Instead of meeting in small groups with lobbyists, they also held controlled "cattle calls" of over 100 lobbyists to share details of the bill. The TCJA proceedings might have revealed the nonprofit sector's lack of political clout, but many more powerful interest groups also felt "steamrolled" by the process, even if they were more satisfied with the results (Vogel and Tankersley, 2017; DeBonis and Werner, 2017; Cary & Holmes, 2019).

9.1.2 Limits of Data and Research

All the advocates interviewed for this Element expressed appreciation for the data and research available to make their case about the likely damage to charitable giving that the tax bill would cause. None regretted the investment sector infrastructure organization had made. But they also acknowledged that it was not adequate to convince policymakers of their case. "What didn't work was very compelling, solid data. We had it. We had the data. And it didn't work," one advocate lamented. Another noted, "I think people are just now starting to realize that if you're that dedicated to denying there's a problem, I'm not sure more data is going to help." A few advocates entertained the possibility that it actually might have helped – that with more data, coming from more independent sources, members of Congress and staff would have been less inclined to dismiss it. The majority, however, didn't have such faith.

They pointed to the variety of ways in which members of Congress and their staff could avoid confronting the case the data made, that charitable giving would decline if the TCJA became law. Some congressional staff simply rejected the sector's research as "fake," or suspect because it came from an interested party, such as the Lilly Family School of Philanthropy. Others pointed out that the data was merely speculative, putting advocates in the difficult position of needing the bill to be passed in order to collect the data necessary to demonstrate the damage it would do. Others conceded the figures but wanted more granular data, which was not yet available, on how the declines in giving would affect their particular districts or favored charities. But by far the most common reason to dismiss the data projecting declining charitable giving stemmed from Republicans' conviction that the TCJA would spur economic growth, which would compensate for any decrease in giving caused by diminished tax incentives. The chairman of the House Ways & Means Committee, Kevin Brady, publicly asserted that charitable giving would actually increase after tax reform.[38]

Advocates' faith in data and research was not shaken by the TCJA setback, but it did illustrate to them that data must be only one part of an advocacy

---

[38] https://independentsector.org/blog/swing-hard-swing-true/

campaign and needed to be accompanied by strong values- and narrative-based messaging and, if possible, information about local impacts.

9.1.3 Hyper-Partisanship

Advocates conceded that their work was made much more difficult by the fact that the TCJA was supported by nearly all Republicans and opposed by all Democrats. "The biggest problem of what happened," argued one advocate, "was that our most recent issues are aligned with a highly partisan bill." This was a problem for several reasons. First, some observers suggested that the partisan nature of the bill's support exposed the weakness of the sectors' influence within the Republican party. "I think there is a heavy weighting to the Democratic side which is not particularly helpful when a Republican-only tax bill is going through the House and the Senate," explained one former congressional staffer with extensive experience working on charitable issues. Sector advocates, outside of the Philanthropy Roundtable, admit being completely taken by surprise by the support for a UCD from Rep. Mark Walker, who, they speculate, was guided by local evangelical groups. Some of the chief champions of charitable giving that the sector had cultivated over the past decade were Democrats, such as Richard Neal (D-Massachusetts) in the House and Chuck Schumer and Ron Wyden (D-Oregon) in the Senate, and they ended up having little power over the bill's fate.

More than this, the pressures of partisanship limited the willingness of both Republicans and Democrats to work closely with sector-wide advocates to improve an imperfect bill. Republicans came to regard any push to modify the bill as an existential political challenge, while advocates suspected that Democrats felt little urgency to address the threats to charitable giving posed by the bill, believing that the damage done would be Republicans' mess to clean up, and that the bill more generally was wholly irredeemable and not worth seeking to improve. Finally, sector advocates also maintained that the partisan nature of the TCJA might have constrained some foundations from aggressively opposing it and instead staying on the sidelines, since doing so would be interpreted as a partisan act.

9.1.4 Disunity

If a single, shared narrative emerged to explain the nonprofit sector advocates' disappointments with the TCJA, besides a general acknowledgment of the sector's lack of "clout," it was the failure of sector advocates to coalesce around agreed-upon strategies and/or objectives. Both advocates and congressional staff commented on this. Several advocates shared a version of a similar story: that they personally had been promoting a strategy that would have likely led to greater success, but that they could not convince their peers to endorse it. That narrative template reflects a shared understanding that the sector did not speak with one voice, and that such divisions undermined their prospects. "Once you have different, opposing remedies floating around out there, nothing gets done," one advocate remarked. "Members of Congress say, if you can't figure it out, if you guys can't decide, then don't expect us to." Another acknowledged, "I think the fair knock on the sector, both in the run-up to 2017 and in the days since … has been that the sector is not aligned around one key ask, one approach."

Some attributed the disunity among sector-wide advocates to exogenous forces, such as the expedited legislative process imposed by Republicans. "We just didn't have time to get on the same page and there was too much disagreement and not enough unanimity," noted one advocate. Others suggested that the "fragmentation of voice" that marred the advocacy campaign was a function of the trade-association-based coalition model, which amplified the fragmenting impulses inherent in the nonprofit sector's commitment to pluralism.

The disunity was most apparent in the advocates' approach to the UCD. Sector advocates and infrastructure group representatives were unable to fully agree on what version of the UCD to unite around – whether the sector should hold out for a "clean" version, or whether it should make concessions to political exigency and throw its weight behind a version with a floor or a cap, which might have a higher chance of passage. Some of the leading charities within the Charitable Giving Coalition were adamantly against a floor, despite its lower costs and compliance burdens, believing the floor would likely be higher than their organizations' median donations.

Sector advocates, for instance, were divided over whether and how strongly to support Rep. Mark Walker's universal charitable deduction bill, introduced in October. For one, Walker's version had a cap of $2,100 for individuals and $4,200 for married couples. But there was also discomfort with partnering with Walker and Sen. Lankford and with some of the bill's key co-sponsors, such as Rep. Mark Meadows (R-North Carolina), a Tea Party stalwart who chaired the House Freedom Caucus. Not only did some sector advocates strongly oppose Meadows' general political allegiances, but Walker, Lankford, and Meadows were all strong supporters of the Johnson Amendment repeal, and some advocates worried that elevating Walker and Lankford as champions of charities would increase repeal's chances. On the other hand, ACR began to work with Walker and other Republican allies and grew frustrated at other advocates' resistance to doing so. Members of the Charitable Giving Coalition who placed a lower priority on the importance of preserving the Johnson Amendment tended to agree with ACR.

In the aftermath of the TCJA's passage, many of these divisions began to come to the surface. Some advocates began to regard the insistence of their Giving Coalition colleagues on a "clean" UCD as a missed opportunity. "In 2017, three to four people in the field pushed so heavily [for the clean UCD] that we didn't get anything," one advocate grumbled. They believed it was an unrealistic ask, given its likely costs. Moreover, they felt that Congress would have been willing to give something more modest to the sector, such as one of the provisions of the 2019 Charity Act, which requires the Treasury to adjust the standard-mileage rate for deducting the use of a personal vehicle for volunteering and made several other changes as well, in an acknowledgment of the damage to charitable giving that the increase to the standard deduction would likely cause.[39] These critiques were not minor quibbles over tactics; they represented fundamental differences over strategic approaches made by sector-wide advocates.

9.2 What Sector-Wide Advocates Learned from the TCJA

No matter what advocates identified as the chief challenges that stymied their work in the TCJA deliberations, there was a broad sense that the experience was instructive. "I think that a lot of quiet lessons were learned in tax reform," conceded one advocate.

Generally speaking, the main takeaway from that experience was that it exposed sector advocates' weakness on the Hill. For all the press releases members of Congress were happy to put out celebrating charities and civil society, that support did not translate into legislative action. As one former staffer summed it up, the TCJA seemed to confirm that, "from the Hill's viewpoint, on a bipartisan basis, members don't really care that much about charities." The TCJA also exposed the significant resentment that many members of Congress felt toward particular nonprofit institutions, such as elite colleges and universities.

Yet despite the widely shared disappointment over the results, some advocates pushed back on too strong an emphasis on defeat. The preservation of the Johnson Amendment was perhaps overshadowed by the failure to secure a universal charitable deduction, but it represented a significant victory nonetheless. Given the limitations imposed directly on other below-the-line deductions within the TCJA, those for state and local taxes and for mortgage interest,

---

[39] https://www.thune.senate.gov/public/_cache/files/ae9e2865-d1b8-464f-bc67-b9c3e44d2068/E2C8B992DFA6C2C57E14853CB20C8350.summary-charity-act-5-15-19-final.pdf

despite active lobbying by a range of other powerful interest groups, the fact that the damage done to the charitable deduction was indirect could be interpreted as a consequence of advocates' efforts over the last decade to convince Congress that the charitable deduction was, in fact, different, more inviolable, than the other two deductions. In this assessment, the outcome of the TCJA might have been bad, but without vigorous sector-wide advocacy, it could have been much, much worse.

That being the case, still, many of the lessons extracted from the TCJA experience involved sector-wide advocacy's shortcomings or missteps. The lack of true congressional champions was keenly felt; some suggested that this had been a surprise in part because the sector had overestimated the depth of its support on the Hill. Nonprofit advocates were so convinced they were representing "the good guys," one acknowledged, that "we got caught with our head in a bag."

Yet in order to attract champions in the future, sector advocates did not seem to feel a need to drastically revise the messaging they had used during the TCJA deliberations. Instead, they more often focused on the need to apply more muscle. For some, this meant to keep doing what they were doing but to do more of it – by, for instance, increasing nonprofit advocates' presence on the Hill with more lobbyists. For others, it suggested the need to reconceive their approach. As one advocate phrased it, "We have to find a way to introduce political risk for elected officials in screwing charities." Another explained: "They didn't fear us. They get to pat us on the head in the meetings and say we support philanthropy and say the right things, but no one thought that if we don't address the charitable deduction then somehow that was going to be a risk to their political career." While for some this imperative reinforced the case for establishing a c4 or PAC to advocate for sector-wide interests, for others it suggested the need to build up a more robust network of allies at the local level willing to push for broad sectoral interests. "I think our target is local charity board members from the business community who are willing to engage with their federal representatives on behalf of charities," one advocate explained. These are people who make significant campaign contributions and who would be willing "to leverage the relationships and capital they have with members of Congress on behalf of charities."

Finally, for some advocates, the TCJA disappointment provoked a reappraisal of the ad hoc interest-group model. They believe that the "fragmentation of voice" that dogged sector-wide advocacy and prevented the formation of a "unified front" was a symptom of structural deficiencies within sector-wide advocacy exacerbated by that model. By definition, as one advocate argued, a trade association approach was necessarily unstable, leading to the fragmentation of constituent stakeholders and contributing to advocates' "divided voice and power." Some suggested that there needed to be a stronger centralizing force that could manage the sort of give-and-take and coalescence around shared aims that might have led to greater success with the TCJA. In any case, nearly all advocates agreed on the need for more local nonprofit leaders actively advocating for the sector's interests, and a tighter coordination of those advocates around a few key talking points and "asks."

10 Post-TCJA Revisions and Reassessments

After the passage of the TCJA, advocates reported a "crisis of confidence in [their] influence as a sector," as one explained. Yet whatever the demoralization experienced by the nonprofit sector in the wake of the TCJA, it proved to be more galvanizing than paralyzing.

The TCJA experience corresponded to a modest increase within several infrastructure organizations of the staff that focused on sector-wide advocacy. More generally, the TCJA had made it clear that the sector needed to further invest in "grasstops" advocacy and to identify locally rooted allies with relationships to key members of Congress. Several groups began to do precisely that. But the TCJA experience also broadened the sector's focus beyond the congressional tax-writing committees, since some of the most vocal champions of charitable giving had been off-committee members like Sen. Lankford and Rep. Walker in part because the tax-writing committees had not been especially receptive. In January 2019, Sen. Lankford was selected to serve on Senate Finance.[40]

Two dynamics spurred additional momentum on sector-wide advocacy after the TCJA's passage. The first was that, once the law was in effect, its shortcomings became more visible, deepening calls for its revision. The second was that, after its passage, the bill's actual, as opposed to hypothetical, impact on charitable giving could be highlighted and wielded as an instrument for promoting the nonprofit sector's priorities.

There was initially some reluctance to take on the revision of the TCJA from both sides of the congressional aisle – from Democrats because the bill's failings served as a useful political cudgel and for Republicans because they hoped to divert attention from those failings more generally. But at least one provision's shortcomings were so glaring that they goaded Congress to act; plus, for some members, endorsing that revision served as a sort of implicit reparative concession that the sector had taken on unintended collateral damage.

---

[40] https://www.lankford.senate.gov/news/press-releases/senator-lankford-selected-to-serve-on-senate-finance-committee

Most significantly, after intense sector-wide lobbying, Congress agreed to roll back a provision that "changed how the unrelated business income tax was applied to nonprofits, resulting in a new 21 percent levy on parking and transportation benefits offered to nonprofit employees" (Daniels, December 17, 2019). Many nonprofits, some of which had never had to pay the UBIT before, were surprised to learn they now had to file tax forms; meanwhile, the tax was exceedingly complicated to implement, with little guidance provided by the IRS. Churches were especially vocal in their protests, and one of the key messaging innovations that led to the provision's repeal was that opponents began to label it "the church parking tax," which carried more bite than the qualified transportation benefit tax. Religious organizations from across the country, including evangelical churches with close relationships to House Republicans, began to complain. In this campaign, they joined the National Council of Nonprofits and a coalition led by the American Society of Association Executives which mobilized more than 600 nonprofits to petition members of Congress to repeal the provision.

Not all nonprofits faced the new tax but those that did were extremely incensed, and the issue-based coalition model harnessed their collective grievance. "We came out of the woodwork on this issue," David Thompson, vice president for public policy at the National Council of Nonprofits, told *the Chronicle of Philanthropy*. "There was a great deal of frustration and genuine anger from nonprofits." Meanwhile, IS bolstered the case against the tax by commissioning a survey from the Urban Institute and George Washington University which determined that the transportation fringe benefits tax would "divert an average of about $12,000 away from each nonprofit's mission per year" (Daniels, 2019).[41]

The campaign proved successful, in part because lawmakers tacitly admitted that they did not realize the provision would affect churches, and a repeal made its way through Congress with little opposition. Not a single Senator or Representative publicly supported keeping the tax. In December 2019, President Trump signed year-end government spending and tax legislation that included the provision's repeal. Although this could be regarded as an unambiguous win for nonprofit sector-wide advocates, some congressional staff pointed out that it should never have gotten that far. The provision had its origins in the 2014 Camp draft tax reform bill, which congressional staff had warned nonprofit advocates might be the source of future legislation and which they called on the sector to scrutinize in order to flag issues that needed to be

---

[41] https://independentsector.org/resource/research-on-ubit-provisions-in-2017-tax-cuts-and-jobs-act/

addressed before that occurred. They suggested that the fact that the provision's inclusion in the TCJA seemed to take sector advocates off-guard was an indictment of those advocates' failure to pursue more forward-looking defensive advocacy.

Another small victory achieved in the same spending package that contained the repeal of the church parking tax was a revision of the private foundation excise tax, from a two-tiered system – 1 percent or 2 percent of net investment income depending on the rate of distributions over the previous five years – to a single, revenue-neutral 1.39 percent rate. The COF had taken the lead in pushing this reform and had managed to get its members to coalesce around the 1.39 percent figure, no mean feat considering that many initially sought to hold out for a lower, single 1 percent rate. Representatives from the Council and other advocates particularly engaged on the issue began a weekly call, outside the aegis of the Charitable Giving Coalition, to coordinate action. The United Philanthropy Forum arranged a campaign by foundations targeting congressional leadership; Rep. Danny Davis (D-Illinois), on House Ways & Means, became an especially vocal champion, but the reform quickly received bipartisan support and was signed into law in December 2019.

Nonprofit advocates had been pursuing the reform for more than a decade, yet there was a range of views as to how significant a victory it should be considered. One advocate described it as a vindication of the single-issue coalition model; the advocate pointed out that the model harnessed the energies of those most committed to working toward reform and argued that if the excise rate revision had been tied to a broader package of reforms, as some advocates were pushing, and as might have been the case in a larger coalition or institution, the revision would have gotten ensnared in other disputed policies. Others, however, made the opposite point: that the 1.39 percent revenue-neutral rate represented a watering-down of sector advocates' aims and that if the policy had been included in a larger reform package, shepherded by infrastructure organization with the entire sector's influence behind it, sector advocates might have been able to achieve the single, lower rate.

The second dynamic, similar to the first, was that after the TCJA's passage, advocates could provide data on its effects that could no longer be dismissed as merely speculative. This data strengthened the case for a UCD and deepened the sense among many policymakers that the current configuration of the charitable deduction was not sustainable. The data highlighted not merely a drop in total charitable giving pegged to the passage of the TCJA – research from the Lilly Family School of Philanthropy and published in *Giving USA 2019 Edition* showed that, adjusted for inflation, total giving declined by 1.7 percent between 2017 and 2018 – but also documented the extent to which the charitable deduction was now claimed by an increasingly small sliver of mostly wealthy taxpayers (Giving USA Foundation, 2019). Research from the Tax Foundation, for instance, showed that in 2019, about 14 percent of taxpayers itemized, compared with 31 percent before the TCJA was enacted (Eastman, September 12, 2019). This egalitarian rationale for the non-itemizer deduction, issued when there were already mounting concerns about the decline of middle- and lower-income donors, joined the more instrumental rationale related to declining aggregate charitable dollars to form a powerful brief on the UCD's behalf.

So, advocates continued their push for an above-the-line charitable deduction, now untethered from the political snares of the TCJA. Their work centered around three bills featuring some version of a UCD moving through Congress: two "clean" versions without a cap, one introduced by Rep. Danny Davis, a member of the House Ways & Means committee, and a bipartisan version introduced by Reps. Henry Cuellar (D-Texas) and Chris Smith (R-New Jersey); and one from Mark Walker with a cap of a third of the standard deduction.[42] The coalition did not throw its weight behind any of them, supporting all as they waited for the larger legislative platform that they would need to be attached to.

But the internal, closed-door debates continued. To assist in them, in 2019, IS commissioned a research report from Indiana's Lilly Family School of Philanthropy, which conducted its study in partnership with the Wharton School of Business at the University of Pennsylvania, on five policy proposals to expand the charitable giving incentives in the tax code and address the declining number of people donating to charity.[43] These included a "clean," non-itemizer charitable deduction; a charitable deduction with a cap; a deduction with a modified 1 percent floor; a nonrefundable 25 percent tax credit; and an "enhanced deduction that provides additional incentives for low- and middle-income taxpayers." For each proposal, the researchers estimated not just the amount of charitable dollars coming in, but also the number of donors it would activate to contribute, and the policy's total cost to the federal government. Together, those three dimensions would help illuminate each policy's impact on American civil society.[44]

The inclusion of a tax credit as a possible policy outcome is worth underscoring because while it is not especially popular among the Washington, DC-advocacy community, it has a significant following among progressive groups

---

[42] https://www.congress.gov/bill/116th-congress/house-bill/1260; https://www.congress.gov/bill/116th-congress/house-bill/651; https://www.congress.gov/bill/116th-congress/house-bill/5293?q=%7B%22search%22%3A%5B%22walker%22%5D%7D&s=7&r=1

[43] https://independentsector.org/resource/impact-of-five-charitable-giving-policy-proposals/

[44] https://independentsector.org/blog/new-research-shows-impact-of-five-charitable-giving-policy-proposals/

around the country as one of the most equitable approaches to incentivizing giving, since it would not disproportionately subsidize the giving of the wealthy. Some advocates actively oppose the credit because they believe that disincentivizing the giving of the wealthy will lead to a decline in charitable revenue for organizations that depend heavily on such giving. In fact, IS received considerable criticism from within the DC-based sector-wide advocacy community for commissioning the report, since some advocates believed that by publicizing the costs to the Treasury attached to the various proposals, and by opening up debate to a broader range of options than the bills making their way through Congress, the report only amplified the fractiousness of the campaign to secure an UCD and undermined its chances on the Hill.

But for IS, that research project better reflected its understanding of its revised role in sector-wide advocacy – and of the potential role for national infrastructure organizations more generally. The shift was both encouraged and provoked by the rise of ad hoc issue-based coalitions. These coalitions' assumption of many of the roles of the traditional trade association freed up space for national infrastructure organizations like IS to double-down on the public interest mandate. For IS, this did not mean abandoning its policy focus; it would continue to be an active participant in sector-wide advocacy campaigns, partnering with the informal coalitions led by a few key national charities and the other sector-wide infrastructure organizations. But its institutional focus would increasingly be not only on short-term policy battles and responses to immediate political threats but on the longer term and bigger picture. It would monitor and seek to protect the health of civil society, broadly conceived, as its recent advocacy for national civic infrastructure attests. It would not merely react to crises and day-to-day political reality but would help to drive the legislative agenda through a process of "collective sense-making" with its members and by its cultivation of the nonprofit research landscape.[45]

It is no accident that equity would be at the center of much of this reconceptualization of sector-wide advocacy. For the centering of equity in considerations of charitable policy, which requires taking seriously the possibilities of trade-offs between members and various stakeholders, sat in some degree of tension with a trade association imperative that seeks to deliver victories for its members. The increased salience of equity in much of IS's work, and to a lesser extent in the COF's activities as well – their policy committee recently decided to take on income inequality as a policy issue – is clearly a reflection of broader

---

[45] https://independentsector.org/blog/the-nonprofit-infrastructure-investment-advocacy-group-is-born/

societal concerns; but it is also a reflection of a reconfigured division of labor and perspectives among sector-wide advocates.

11 Sector-Wide Advocacy in Response to the COVID-19 Crisis

In the aftermath of the TCJA, the National Council of Nonprofits came to believe that one path to securing a permanent, non-itemizer deduction might be through the institution of a temporary one as part of emergency disaster legislation. It proposed disaster relief legislation that would be automatically triggered with a declaration of a national disaster and that would include a time-bound, targeted, non-itemizer deduction. The hope was that, once installed temporarily, it would become easier to extend permanently. The IRA charitable rollover provides a precedent; it first passed as a temporary provision in a relief bill for Hurricane Katrina in 2004–2005 before it was made permanent at the end of 2015.

Of course, NCN could have had no sense how prescient that plan would prove. The coronavirus created an emergency of massive scale that would make tremendous demands on nonprofits and sector-wide advocacy, but also provide significant opportunities.

In many respects, the maturation of the ad hoc coalitions during the TCJA deliberations set up sector advocates to move quickly in response to the coronavirus crisis. Soon after the likely scale of the pandemic became clear in March 2020, and as Congress was deliberating over what would become its first COVID-relief response, leading sector-wide advocates, including representatives from IS, NCN, and many of the largest national charities that had been most active in the Charitable Giving Coalition, began to plan strategy and coordinate a response.[46] They held early morning phone calls, with as many as two dozen advocates participating, seven days a week. It's a testament to the dominance of this advocacy model that the locus of so much of COVID-related nonprofit advocacy does not have an official name, to say nothing of official infrastructure or designated staff. Participants sometimes call themselves members of the 7:30 Coffee Club. Before long, a second afternoon call was added, to accommodate the growing interest among nonprofit organizations, with at times up to a hundred participants. By the end of the summer of 2020, the frequency of calls lessened to three days a week. Advocates identified the primary challenges faced by nonprofits as well as their main priorities in addressing the pandemic and strategized how to elevate them in Congress's deliberations over the next COVID-relief package.

---

[46] https://www.dol.gov/agencies/whd/pandemic/ffcra-employee-paid-leave

As Congress debated the details of this package, which would become the Coronavirus Aid, Relief, and Economic Security (CARES) Act, the coalition ultimately coalesced around a number of key "asks." Among them were $60 billion in emergency relief funding for nonprofits, what one advocate described as a "big audacious number to get Congress's attention"; granting nonprofits access to the emergency, and potentially forgivable, Small Business Administration's Paycheck Protection Program (PPP) loans; and the creation of a universal charitable deduction for all charitable donations after March 1, 2020, to stimulate additional charitable giving. The ultimate message was that the congressional COVID relief/stimulus package needed to have a strong nonprofit and civil society component.

The message was partially received. Overall, advocates regarded the CARES Act as a significant win, if not as an absolute triumph. One rated its passage as a seven out of ten for the sector but pointed out that this was about as high on the scale as they had reached in recent years. Nonprofits were made eligible for PPP loans for up to $10 million, but only those with under 500 employers were eligible. In the Senate version of the bill, nonprofits would have been ineligible for the loans if they had received Medicaid payments; sector advocates furiously pushed back and this provision was not included in the final bill. One study estimated that the PPP loan program saved 4.1 million nonprofit jobs, roughly a third of all nonprofit jobs in the United States (Parks, 2020). The bill also lifted the cap on annual giving that can be deducted from taxable income from 60 percent of adjusted gross income to 100 percent. Finally, a non-itemizer deduction of up to $300 in cash was added for the 2020 tax year, with strict penalties for abuse. Given the disappointments of the TCJA, this last provision was a point of particular pride for sector-wide advocates, even though they had hoped for a larger allowed deduction amount. "When the pandemic hit, because of all that grunt work of the past two years," noted one advocate, "when the CARES Act came together, the UCD was part of the conversation."

Yet, it also became clear that many of these provisions were poorly designed with respect to nonprofits; they were in a sense "tacked on" to the existing legislation, creating imperfect fits between the reality of nonprofit needs during the pandemic and the federal relief bureaucracy. Nonprofits, and especially smaller ones, struggled with confusing eligibility requirements; reports trickled in of nonprofits being confronted with forms for loans that asked who the "owner" of the firm was. Nonprofit sector-wide advocates worked to alert government officials to these issues while also ensuring that they were addressed in the possible subsequent round of congressional pandemic-related stimulus (Theis, 2020).

In the midst of the pandemic, person-to-person lobbying was nearly impossible. So, advocates turned to other means. In mid-March 2020, the coalition issued a public letter, signed by the leaders of forty national nonprofits, stressing the need to include support for nonprofits as a key element of any governmental response to the crisis. Over the next few weeks, the informal coalition added more than 200 signatories urging the inclusion of advocates' key asks in the CARES Act. With guidance from the National Council of Nonprofits, state associations were encouraged to adapt the letter and send it to local representatives.

Advocates noted several significantly improved dynamics in their work compared to the lobbying campaign during the TCJA deliberations. First, many of those interviewed noted how much better sector advocates worked together. In part, this was because many members of the group had developed working relationships during the TCJA deliberations as well as a productive division of labor. In fact, the COVID-relief coalition developed an even more sophisticated structure than the Charitable Giving Coalition, with the generation of specialized subgroups. A group of communications professionals began to meet regularly, for instance, to discuss a coordinated public relations strategy. So too did a group dedicated to state and local issues. The COVID-relief coalition was even more broadly constructed than the Charitable Giving Coalition, and aimed for a degree of representation legitimacy. But like with the Charitable Giving Coalition, a core, tightly knit group drove the process, with other organizations dropping in and out as they saw fit. It's also possible that the severity of the crisis encouraged more comity and coalescence. "The sector, particularly around COVID, has been as united as it's ever been and has been very clear on our priorities. And it's been much easier to convey our concerns to the Hill," commented one advocate.

The second dynamic was a rising pool of potential "champions" willing to promote nonprofit interests in COVID legislation. In part this could be attributed to the ways in which the pandemic underscored key elements of the case that nonprofit advocates had been making for years, making it abundantly clear how vital nonprofits were to the safety and security of communities across the United States. Nonprofit employees emerged as key "essential workers" and "frontline responders" as demand for their services mounted, while at the same time, they faced dire financial prospects due to lost revenue. In a sense, social service and health nonprofits – the organizations that, according to advocates, politicians most vividly associated with and valued as charities – powerfully stood in for the sector as a whole. As the affirmative case for prioritizing nonprofits became easier to make, nonprofit advocates spoke less frequently about the need to "introduce political risk" into their lobbying, which would somehow instill fear in politicians about crossing nonprofits.

Indeed, even more of the "grasstops" advocacy that sector-wide advocates had long promoted began to occur organically, as nonprofit leaders from across the country contacted their representatives to urge them to support nonprofit relief. This, for instance, is how Rep. Seth Moulton (D-Massachusetts) was initially recruited to the cause. The head of a large YMCA in his district reached out to him to let him know the extent to which the organization was struggling to meet the immense demand in the North Shore region of Massachusetts, with its financial resources potentially drying up. Rep. Moulton asked his staff to look into what could be done; they reached out to a national infrastructure organization that had contacted the office earlier, which laid out the advocates' key requests. This led Rep. Moulton to actively take up the nonprofit cause. He circulated a letter, written with Rep. Brian Fitzpatrick (R-Pennsylvania), and signed by more than 140 members of Congress, calling on Congress to support nonprofits in COVID relief. Moulton also introduced a bill, co-sponsored by Fitzpatrick, the Save Organizations that Serve America Act, that addressed many of the sector's demands.[47] It called for assisting nonprofits with $60 billion of funding, making the universal charitable deduction's inclusion in the CARES Act permanent, and removing the 500-employee cap on nonprofits qualified to apply for PPP loans, among other provisions.

In May 2020, a bipartisan group of thirty senators signed a letter to the Senate leadership calling for the removal of the 500-employee cap for PPP loans, an increase in unemployment insurance reimbursement for self-funded nonprofits, and an expansion of the UCD passed in the CARES Act.[48] They also called for allowing charitable donations made in the five months after the declaration of national emergency in mid-March to be deducted from 2019 tax filings. In early June, the Charitable Giving Coalition helped arrange a conference call with a bipartisan group of six senators, three Republicans (Sens. Lankford, Tim Scott [R-South Carolina], and Mike Lee [R-Utah], the first two of whom served on Senate Finance) and three Democrats (Sens. Coons [D-Delaware], Shaheen [D-New Hampshire], and Klobuchar [D-Minnesota]) in which they sang the praises of the work nonprofits were doing to address the COVID crisis, making sure to stress the strong bipartisan nature of their support, and called for an extension and expansion of the $300 universal charitable deduction. Later in the

---

[47] https://moulton.house.gov/press-releases/moulton-fitzpatrick-142-other-members-of-congress-and-nations-leading-nonprofits-urge-house-leadership-to-support-relief-for-americas-nonprofits; https://moulton.house.gov/press-releases/moulton-and-fitzpatrick-introduce-the-save-organizations-that-serve-america-act-to-include-charitable-nonprofits-in-economic-relief

[48] https://www.lankford.senate.gov/imo/media/doc/Nonprofit%20Support%20Letter%20to%20Leadership.pdf

month, these senators introduced a bill that would do precisely that.[49] The public support that nonprofits received from these and other senators in the months after the pandemic struck represented one of the most impressive demonstrations of congressional champions in recent memory.

Yet the advocates' momentum stalled in the second half of 2020, with the House emerging as a particular roadblock. Ultimately, the relief package that Congress passed in December 2020 ended up being a mixed bag for the sector. It extended the non-itemizer charitable deduction to 2021 but kept the amount at $300, although it allowed for a $600 deduction for couples.[50] It also provided nonprofits access to the second round of PPP loans, but made the eligibility criteria even more restrictive than in the CARES Act, lowering the employee cap to 300, so that thousands of nonprofits that qualified for the first round would no longer qualify for the second. Yet, if disappointed with some of the details, sector-wide advocates were not nearly as demoralized as in the aftermath of the TCJA, buoyed by a sense that real progress had been made. "If you had asked me a year ago, where we would be today – putting aside the pandemic," one advocate remarked in late November. "I would be very happy from just a pure policy perspective to be where we are at. I'd be thrilled." The authors of this Element can confirm that, when asked about the prospects of a universal charitable deduction in the months before the pandemic struck, many advocates were not optimistic even a modest one could get passed.[51]

12 Sector-Wide Advocacy and Philanthropic Reform

The recent surge in calls for philanthropic reform represents a final dimension of legislative action around which the balance between contending missions and organizational structures of nonprofit sector-wide advocacy must be struck. Such calls have been mounting for years – the product of a series of high-profile controversies surrounding private foundations; the attention being paid to new developments in the sector, such as the meteoric rise of DAFs; and the growth of mega-philanthropy, which has attracted increased public, and often critical, scrutiny. The pandemic and its convergence with protests over racial justice have only amplified those calls, which have been channeled into demands to get money into the hands of frontline charities as quickly as possible. This, in turn, has led to several advocacy campaigns directed toward

---

[49] https://www.lankford.senate.gov/news/press-releases/lankford-leads-bipartisan-group-to-introduce-bill-expanding-federal-tax-deduction-for-charitable-giving

[50] https://independentsector.org/blog/congress-last-minute-deal-leaves-mixed-results-for-nonprofits/

[51] See also Parks and Theis (2020); Daniels and Theis (2020).

regulations to increase payout rules for DAFs and private foundations (Daniels, May 13, 2020).[52]

Philanthropic reform poses particular challenges for sector-wide advocacy because it threatens to expose fault lines within the nonprofit sector: between funding organizations and grantees, between large and small nonprofits, and between organizations that rely heavily on private giving for revenue and those that do not. There are two ways to address these divisions, corresponding to the decentralized and more centralized models discussed in Section 8. Actors can fragment around different issue-based coalitions that separately promote their individual interests; or those interests could be brought together under the aegis of a more centralized institution where compromises and trade-offs between them could be managed.

In the past, infrastructure and advocacy groups have pursued a mix of these approaches. Given the general opposition of foundations to these reforms, many nonprofit advocacy groups have shied away from such issues, nervous about alienating potential donors. This was, for instance, the lesson that some sector-wide advocates learned from supporting the push to disallow foundations from counting administrative expenses toward their mandated payouts, part of the Charitable Giving Act of 2003.[53] Some have responded to calls for philanthropic reform as a threat to the institutional interests of their members and supporters and mobilized against them, as traditional trade associations might.[54] In fact, the rise of reform attention directed to DAFs, at the state and federal level, has led to a compensatory defensive response from both established and new entrants in the sector-wide advocacy landscape (Haynes, January 1, 2020). Finally, sector-wide advocates and infrastructure organizations have sought to work as mediators between various interests or as a central negotiator with policymakers, as occurred in the run-up to the Pension Protection Act.

Some nonprofit advocates called on infrastructure organizations and some of the major philanthropic foundations to take on this more engaged role; that is, they assumed that philanthropic reform would occur at some point in the not-too-distant future and thought that reform would be better designed if it reflected the involvement of sector-wide advocates who had the clout – and the resources – to speak broadly for the sector. They also worried that if established advocacy and infrastructure organizations and major foundations did not stake reformist ground as their appropriate territory, others would do so in their place.

---

[52] http://charitystimulus.org/
[53] https://www.ncrp.org/2015/11/when-rick-cohen-led-ncrp.html
[54] https://www.bc.edu/content/dam/bc1/schools/law/centers/philanthropy/09_06_2017-DAF-Joint-Response.pdf

In fact, one of the most striking developments over the last several years within the realm of philanthropic reform has been the active role that individual large-scale donors, such as Kat Taylor and John Arnold, have played in pushing it. Their involvement raises important questions about how these individual donors with significant resources at their disposal fit into the existing advocacy landscape, and to what extent they will serve as allies with or rivals to existing, more established institutional actors.

John Arnold's Initiative to Accelerate Charitable Giving, developed in partnership with Boston College law professor Ray Madoff, highlights many of these dynamics.[55] The initiative, which has no staff or official institutional apparatus behind it, calls for reforms to incentivize faster payout of DAFs and private foundation funds, among other provisions. To some extent, the Initiative can be considered yet another of the informal issue-based coalitions that have defined much sector-wide advocacy over the last decade. But it is also one that has more allegiance to the public interest mandate of advocacy than the trade association model.

There are several dynamics within the Initiative worth noting for what they suggest about future developments within sector-wide advocacy. First and most obvious is the prominent role played by an individual donor in partnership with an individual activist, outside the bounds of established infrastructure or advocacy organizations, an illustration of the centrifugal forces shaping the field. Second, the Initiative won public support from a handful of major philanthropic foundations, including Ford, Kellogg, Kresge, and Hewlett, among others, with some additional major foundations playing a more behind-the-scenes, supporting role. This represents a major step in sector-wide advocacy; a consistent complaint from many sector-wide advocates was the reluctance of foundations to publicly engage in sector-wide issues, relinquishing an opportunity to exert their influence. It also might reassure some nonprofit advocacy groups that they can embrace philanthropic reform without the fear of losing philanthropic funding. Third, the Initiative melded together payout reform with calls for enhanced charitable incentives to increase the amount of charitable giving and the number of donors, calling specifically for a non-itemizer deduction with a floor, set at a percentage of AGI. This suggests the possibility of a broader package in which philanthropic reform is coupled with charitable giving incentives, echoing the similar mixture of carrot-and-sticks in the Pension Protection Act. As of now, advocates are not reporting signs of such "crossing of the streams" on Capitol Hill, with lawmakers holding off on supporting incentives until reforms are imposed. But such a give-and-take is a possibility, given the history of sector-wide advocacy.

---

[55] https://acceleratecharitablegiving.org/

In June 2021, Senators Angus King (I-Maine) and Chuck Grassley introduced legislation that contained several of the reforms proposed by the Initiative to Accelerate Charitable Giving, the Accelerating Charitable Efforts (ACE) Act.[56] The major, sector-wide infrastructure organizations – Philanthropy Roundtable, Independent Sector, United Philanthropy Forum, COF, and Community Foundation Public Awareness Initiative – signed a letter expressing concern about the legislation, suggesting that the contest over the ACE Act is not merely one over a particular vision of philanthropic reform, but also over which kinds of organizations and individuals take the lead in sector-wide advocacy.

The prospects of the legislation are uncertain at the moment. But if momentum does begin to build for significant philanthropic reform in Congress, it will present a test for the contending models and missions of nonprofit sector advocacy. Not that they will necessarily be in direct competition; the greater the chance of reform, the more essential the trade association model will become in beating it back or in defending the institutional interest of DAF-sponsoring organizations and private foundations, while the need for a mediating and brokering institution that takes into consideration the needs of civil society from a broader perspective will also be underscored. It is even possible that a major philanthropic reform, if it arrives, will help cement a sort of longer-term *modus operandi* between these two models of nonprofit sector-wide advocacy, a balance between centripetal and centrifugal forces.

13 State- and Local-Level Advocacy on Sector-Wide Issues

As acknowledged in Section 3.2, while federal sector-wide advocacy is the focus in this Element, state and, to some extent, local advocacy also has an important bearing on nonprofit activities. Table 1 and Section 3.2 describe some important, state- and some local-level sector-wide issues. Interviewees pointed to state nonprofit associations as the most important organizations undertaking sector-wide advocacy at the state level. These membership associations vary greatly in size and strength from state to state, and advocacy work often takes second place to providing capacity-building assistance to member nonprofits. Many state associations rely more heavily on foundation grant support than member dues for their income. This is so in part because the associations generally attract a modest percentage of state nonprofits as dues-paying members and must contend with nonprofits' deeper interest in subsector rather than sector-wide issues and the modest budgets of many nonprofits. However, an

---

[56] https://www.king.senate.gov/newsroom/press-releases/king-grassley-introduce-legislation-to-ensure-charitable-donations-reach-working-charities

attraction of association membership is that the associations can provide political cover for individual nonprofits who may be concerned with alienating state funders with their own advocacy, and the sector-wide associations can also attend to issues that cut across nonprofit subsectors. State nonprofit associations can be joined by statewide United Way coalitions, regional associations of grantmakers and some individual foundations, state human service associations, and other statewide subsector groups as allies in sector-wide advocacy, with variation in the specific line-up of sector advocates from issue to issue and state to state.

While state advocates are closer to the grassroots than their federal counterparts, nevertheless state like federal advocates rely more heavily on grasstops than grassroots advocacy strategies. State-like federal advocates also often find themselves doing more defensive advocacy, trying to stop unfavorable policy from being enacted, than proactive policy advocacy. Interviewees reported that crises affecting nonprofits can help bring different types of nonprofits together to advocate on sector-wide issues. Interviewees also suggested that state-level sector advocates have become more diverse and stronger in recent decades, but that they still have modest influence compared to unions (which are part of the overall tax-exempt sector) and the small business community, let alone big business. State association leaders called for more resources for advocacy, and also recommended more coordination of federal, state, and local advocacy efforts. With the dearth of analysis of state-level sector-wide advocacy (for some exceptions, see Coble, 1999; Alvarado, 2000; and Balassiano and Chandler, 2010), there is also a need for more study of this phenomenon that can help inform reform efforts.

14 Recommendations for Enhancing Sector-Wide Advocacy

In reflecting on events over the past decade, our interviewees offered numerous suggestions for strengthening nonprofit sector-wide advocacy. Many of these recommendations were touched on briefly in various sections of this Element. They are collected and discussed further here, along with elaboration from the authors that build on the interview material.

14.1 Increase Resources for Federal-Level, Nonprofit Sector-Wide Advocacy

According to most of those we talked with, devoting more resources to federal-level, nonprofit sector-wide advocacy is a starting point for strengthening this advocacy. Increased resources for sector-wide advocacy could come either from infrastructure organizations allocating a greater share of their existing funds and staff to this advocacy or from their raising additional, new funding for this activity. While it is impossible to determine what the ideal amount to spend on advocacy is, it seems clear, for example, that spending for nonprofit sector-wide advocacy lags significantly behind spending for business sector-wide advocacy, even accounting for the differences in the sizes of the two sectors and the tendency of some nonprofits to understate their lobbying expenses to avoid IRS scrutiny for excessive spending on this activity (Boris and Maronick, 2012). As shown in Table 2, in 2017, the year the TCJA was enacted, spending on lobbying as reported by major sector-wide organizations from the business sector was more than 235 times greater than similar spending by nonprofit sector-wide advocates, which again may be somewhat understated. As also shown in the table, business sector-wide lobbying staffing (284 staff) similarly greatly outnumbered nonprofit sector-wide staffing (17 staff), and, notably, business sector-wide advocacy associations devoted a much larger percentage of their much larger budgets to lobbying (45.7 percent) than similar nonprofit associations (1.9 percent). In comparison, for many years the business sector has contributed approximately fifteen times as much to the US economy as the nonprofit sector, and business has accounted for roughly ten times the wage and salary accruals as the nonprofit sector (McKeever et al., 2016).

14.2 Mobilize Grasstops

As noted in the body of the Element, sector-wide advocates identified a grasstops strategy, in which local nonprofit executives and influential board members are mobilized to contact their members of Congress in support of sector-wide issues, as one of the more effective approaches to advocacy. Unfortunately, for a variety of reasons, the nonprofit sector has not been able to take full advantage of this strategy. One major reason is that several national advocates are only indirectly connected – or not connected at all – to local notables, like nonprofit executives and board members, who care about the nonprofit sector and might have some clout with federal policymakers.

At best, the template of recent years seems to be to rally local resources in times of threat or crisis, like attempts to overturn the Johnson Amendment, to good effect, only to have them demobilize afterward. Is there a mechanism that can be used to more regularly flex this muscle which would keep sector-wide issues on the radar of the congressional representatives of local charities, and make mass mobilization more effective in times of future sector-wide crises?

Table 2 Lobbying staff and expenses and total expenses of nonprofit and business sector-wide associations, 2017.

Sector-wide associations	Total expenses	Lobbying expenses	Lobbying expenses as % of total expenses	Lobbying staff
Nonprofit				
Council on Foundations	$13,642,985	$220,000	1.6%	5
Independent Sector	$8,621,594	$46,000	0.5%	4
National Council of Nonprofits	1,713,662	$110,000	6.4%	3
Philanthropy Roundtable	$8,917,853	$280,000	3.1%	5
United Philanthropy Forum[a]	$2,428,962	$6,300	0.3%	NA
Total, nonprofit	$35,325,056	$662,300	1.9%	17
Business				
Business Roundtable	$49,287,729	$27,400,000	5.6%	65
National Association of Manufacturers	$46,062,573	$8,100,000	17.6%	30
National Federation of Independent Business[a]	$89,045,963	$39,698,062	44.6%	20
US Chamber of Commerce[b]	$160,435,832	$82,300,000	51.3%	169
Total, business	$344,832,097	$157,498,062	45.7%	284

[a] Lobbying expenses from 990 form.
[b] Includes lobbying expenses for four subsidiaries.

Sources: Total expenses from 990 forms from Candid, guidestar.org; lobbying expenses and staffing from Center for Responsive Politics, opensecrets.org

In the case of the nonprofit response to COVID and the subsequent lobbying over the CARES Act, the nonprofit sector benefitted from the recent experience of the TCJA fights. But what if there is a longer gap between legislative crises and opportunities? If local grasstops are among the most effective spokespeople for the nonprofit sector and those for whom congressional allies have the greatest affinity, what can be done to maintain grasstop engagement in noncrisis times? Is there a formal or informal mechanism that could be set up to prioritize congressional relationships? How can grasstops best be made to understand that this needs to be at least a second-tier priority? Is this something that could be handled with routine Zoom check-ins or monthly phone calls to keep national sector-wide issues visible for local nonprofit leaders or is a more formal structure needed? Could more local nonprofits have designated policy liaisons who dedicate, if not their full time, then at least some segment of it to staying plugged into national sector-wide advocacy year-round? To be sure, some efforts have now begun to take up these activities, but they need to be intensified and given even more resources.

The emphasis on the value of grasstops advocacy is not meant to entirely discount the contribution that grassroots strategy could also make to sector-wide advocacy. A grassroots approach seeks to mobilize ordinary citizens, including those who benefit from nonprofit services, and not just the local nonprofit leaders and board members that grasstops advocacy aims to activate. The strengths of a grassroots strategy are the potential for engaging large numbers of individuals in contacting policymakers in support of preferred policies, including new, different, and more diverse voices that may be part of grasstops efforts. The overall public fondness for the nonprofit sector and the declining cost of reaching large numbers of citizens through social media add to the appeal of a grassroots strategy.

At the same time, there are significant challenges in expanding grassroots advocacy on sector-wide issues. These are often relatively complicated tax and regulatory issues that are not likely to ignite the passions of the general public and motivate them to vote for one political candidate or another, write or call their members of Congress, or take to the street to demonstrate, which are the kinds of activities that would get the attention of policymakers. No sector-wide advocacy organizations currently seem set up to do grassroots advocacy on sector-wide issues, and developing this capacity would take the kind of resources that are not currently abundant in the sector-wide advocacy community. Overall, expanding grassroots advocacy on sector-wide issues seems worth exploring, but it may not be the highest priority for advocates right now.

14.3 Dedicate Funding Support for New, Sector-Wide Advocates

Would it be possible to organize a pool of money at one or more foundations that would fund distributed positions in local nonprofits dedicated to sector-wide advocacy? If staffing in this area is a primary problem, could support be generated for a standing "Policy Liaison Officer" program in which a fund and/or foundations pay for embedded positions at different nonprofits? The liaison officer's job would be to interact with and support their counterparts at other local organizations to generate coordinated action on sector-wide issues. Some of the leading national charities have dedicated advocacy personnel, but would there not be a benefit to extending this to medium-sized or even smaller entities to help develop more commonality in the nonprofit sector-wide approach to legislative priorities? What are possible funding sources for such a program? At the same time, care must be taken to adhere to regulations forbidding foundation earmarking of funds for lobbying.

14.4 Codify Legislative Relationship Maps

Returning to the idea that the sector as a whole tends to lapse its focus on legislative relationships when there is no crisis, it's worth pushing for the continuation of the documentation of relationship maps following major legislative advocacy efforts. It seems that a standing database of contacts, allies, and local champions in districts represented by key legislators would be a useful tool, even beyond what has been started. There is perhaps a modest objection that formally setting this type of information down in a database risks compromising relationships that are built on trust and personal connections. The counter-argument is that some sort of record of these relationships forces a focus on their cultivation, particularly in times of noncrisis, and ensures continuity as the leadership of organizations changes. Ideally, this would be something nonprofits could sign up to access and contribute to for free, the better to promote the sharing of information.

14.5 Encourage Governmental Research to Increase Congressional Knowledge of the Value of the Nonprofit Sector

To bridge the divide between the nonprofit sector needing to advocate for itself and it also not wanting to "sully its image" in doing so, sector-wide advocates might encourage more frequent, organic analyses from within Congress or other parts of the government on the nonprofit sector's role and the potential impacts of legislation on its functioning. For example, it seems that the last publicly available Congressional Research Service (CRS) report on the nonprofit sector was released in 2009 (Sherlock and Gravelle, 2009). Are there allies on the Hill who could ask CRS to revisit the nonprofit sector with an eye to examining and hopefully illuminating its positive impact on US society and the economy, particularly during COVID? That seems like one way to generate independent analyses of the sector's utility without having to peddle reports generated by nonprofits themselves. Obviously, encouraging assessments by CRS, the Congressional Budget Office, the Government Accountability Office, the Bureau of Labor Statistics, the Census Bureau, or other government agencies risks there being some aspect of an assessment that is unfavorable, but it also presents an opportunity to inform policymakers completely free of the perception of self-interested lobbying.

14.6 Identify the Next Challenge

Although TCJA was eventually seen largely as a defeat for nonprofits, sector-wide advocates had done some things before action on TCJA in 2017 to prepare themselves for tax reform. What is the next major legislative event that needs to be prepared for now? What is the potential "seismic event" that could negatively impact charitable giving – or alternately create markedly more positive prospects? How can public and private research organizations be best engaged to examine these challenges and opportunities? Promoting discussion within the sector on this topic – and ideally building consensus – would help clarify where study and research dollars can best be applied. As seen in recent legislative campaigns, data and research had limited utility to change minds among hardened congressional opponents, but they did prove to be useful in bolstering the position of allies and amplifying their voices.

14.7 Develop and Vet "PreFabricated" Legislative Asks

It is an unfortunate truth that disaster relief legislation has been an avenue for introducing provisions that promote charitable giving. Having proactive legislation "on the shelf" in the event of an unexpected legislative opening is therefore a sensible strategy for sector-wide advocates. The benefit of this tactic was seen in the inclusion of a non-itemizer deduction in the COVID-relief bill, with the hope that such a step could lead to the provision eventually becoming permanent. This follows on the precedent of introducing the IRA rollover as part of the aid package in response to Hurricane Katrina. Obviously, if such asks are to be optimized, they shouldn't be created on the fly in the moment of crisis. Thought is therefore needed sector-wide on what next steps could best benefit nonprofits and what form the legislative language should take. Having "pre-baked" options could facilitate leveraging future legislative relief packages to incorporate useful provisions in law – either on a temporary or permanent basis.

Given the sensitivity of this tactic, some level of sector-wide consensus is needed to ensure that whatever the next emergency ask is, it enjoys widespread sector support.

14.8 Ask Tough Questions about How to Accommodate Hyper-Partisanship

How can nonprofit sector-wide advocates better balance the appeal to Republicans of nonprofits as alternatives to government action with the perception of the sector as dominated by Democratic-leaning staff and leaders? Moreover, how can the sector do this at a time when the Republican Party itself is rife with internal divisions? On the one hand, there is a Trumpist faction that seemingly embraces polarization and might be happy to fixate on the nonprofit sector's perceived partisan bias.[57] On the other is a more accommodating traditional wing, that sees appeal in the utility of charity, heirs to Bush Sr.'s "thousand points of light." Is reaching out to that traditional wing dangerous as it might further alienate the Trumpist wing – which at least as of this writing looks like it is still a strong force in the party? Is papering over partisan disconnects simply an impossibility so long as the Republican Party is at war with itself? Does this discussion also risk an unwelcome revival of the Johnson Amendment debate?

14.9 Develop a Legislative Vanguard

A fundamental challenge for the nonprofit sector seems to be that the more it overtly presses for its interests, the more it negatively affects the positive image most Americans and Congress have of it. How does the sector retain the veneer of disinterested service to the public good while doing the dirty work of campaigning for its special interests? Is one way to carve out a specific legislative-focused entity whose job and identity would be to engage in the bare-knuckles aspects of effecting positive legislative changes? There would, of course, have to be a connection with the more well-regarded aspects of the nonprofit sector, such as food banks, homeless shelters, and medical clinics. The vanguard would leverage the good work of these charities while keeping them out of the direct line of fire.

Obviously, this is just a general notion – and one that leaves many questions unanswered – such as exactly how would the vanguard connect with the mass of nonprofits and draw on their influential grasstops and other political resources? And, who would be the main funding source for this new organization and who

---

[57] See, for instance, comments made by then Ohio Republican Senate candidate J. D. Vance (*Philanthropy Daily*, 2021).

would influence what its priorities are? Or is it narrowly focused on two or three goals, like UCD, with specific objectives baked into its founding charter? Could it take the form of a PAC or a 501(c)(4), although these options have so far not gained wide support within the nonprofit sector? Even if it is ultimately deemed an unworkable idea, the prospect of such a vanguard organization could serve as an interesting strawman to put out there to generate discussion on how the sector moves forward, at least in trying to focus discussion on sector-wide advocacy versus the pull of subsector priorities.

One key question is whether such an organization is more viable if it is focused exclusively on defensive lobbying efforts. Is it easier to generate support for such an entity if its sole goal is to prevent legislative actions that harm the sector's interests, rather than pushing for proactive changes that may not have sector-wide support?

If the "vanguard" is a preferred approach, is there a past model to build on? Should it be an existing leadership organization on steroids or a more permanent and muscular version of the Charitable Giving Coalition? Or is a fresh-sheet-of-paper approach needed for introducing a new, standing legislative advocacy body into the nonprofit sector?

Or is a *laissez-faire* approach better? One that preserves the nobility of the sector's image without a centralizing force fighting on its behalf on a permanent basis? The alternative is to just assume that "good will out" when it's needed and that if the nonprofit sector does its work well, leaders will naturally emerge and be there when legislative crises require them, possibly with more credibility than the "nonprofit vanguard." But is this approach simply too risky? What if the right people aren't in the right place at the right time?

15 Conclusion

So, what to make of the current moment with respect to nonprofit sector-wide advocacy? If the TCJA experience should not be reduced to an absolute defeat for sector advocates, the COVID-19 crisis cannot be understood as an absolute triumph. The indeterminacy confronted when assessing the effectiveness of sector-wide advocacy in each of these cases prevents a complete vindication of any one model or approach. What nonprofit sector-wide advocacy seems to have arrived at now is an uneasy, working equilibrium between the two dominant models that have developed over the last decade. Issue-based informal coalitions, focused on short-term, if vital, legislative campaigns, are now precariously balanced against the public good mandate embraced by IS and to some extent by the COF, which attends to longer time horizons, a broad conception of the defense of civil society, and more recently, the promotion of the ideal of equity.

This balance was born out of the disappointments of the TCJA and then developed in the midst of a worldwide pandemic. Can it be maintained as the crisis subsides? Will it deliver enough for individual institutions, either in terms of charitable incentives or the pushing back of philanthropic reform? Will it be cohesive enough to promote an affirmative ideal of civil society to meet longer-term needs and address broader societal trends – or to help orchestrate a broader package of reform? Will the newly created champions that have emerged during the COVID crisis, both in Congress and among nonprofits around the nation, continue their support for sector-wide issues into the future?

Several other questions present themselves as well. Will the informal coalitions continue to develop more sophistication, moving closer to institutionalization? How will the efforts of individual major donors to reform philanthropy or nonprofits be incorporated into the existing nonprofit sector-wide advocacy landscape? Will any new institutions be necessary to promote the existing balance between ad hoc coalitions and established infrastructure groups, or will existing institutions need to be revised in significant ways? How should philanthropic support for nonprofit sector-wide advocacy from foundations or individual donors adapt to the developments over the last few years in light of these pressing questions?

If the answers to these questions are not immediately clear, what does seem obvious is that the current configuration of nonprofit sector-wide advocacy is a dynamic one, still not fully cooled and congealed after the tumult of the TCJA and the crisis of COVID-19. This means there will surely be much grappling with the fundamental nature of nonprofit sector advocacy and the organizational and institutional arrangements that best serve these purposes in the years to come.

References

Abramson, A. J. (2016). Making Public Policy toward the Nonprofit Sector in the U.S.: How and Why Broad, "Sector" Interests Are Advanced – or Not – in Federal Policymaking. *Nonprofit Policy Forum* 7(2), 257–284. https://doi.org/10.1515/npf-2015-0050.

Abramson, A. J. & McCarthy, R. (2012). Infrastructure Organizations. In L. M. Salamon, ed. *The State of Nonprofit America*. 2nd ed. Washington, DC: Brookings Institution Press, pp. 423–458.

Alvarado, A. (2000). State-Level Policy: Growing Role for Nonprofit Associations. *Nonprofit Quarterly*, September 21. https://nonprofitquarterly.org/state-level-policy-growing-role-for-nonprofit-associations/.

Arnsberger, P., Ludlum, M., Riley, M., & Stanton, M. (2008). A History of the Tax-Exempt Sector: An SOI Perspective. *Statistics of Income Bulletin* 27(3): 105–135. www.irs.gov/pub/irs-soi/08winbul.pdf.

Balassiano, K. & Chandler, S. M. (2010). The Emerging Role of Nonprofit Associations in Advocacy and Public Policy: Trends, Issues, and Prospects. *Nonprofit and Voluntary Sector Quarterly* 19(5): 946–955. https://journals-sagepub-com.mutex.gmu.edu/doi/10.1177/0899764009338963.

Bokoff, J., McGill, L., Nylen-Wysocki, E., & Wolcheck, D. (2018). U.S. Foundation Funding for Nonprofit and Philanthropic Infrastructure, 2004–2015. Foundation Center and William & Flora Hewlett Foundation. www.issuelab.org/resources/32151/32151.pdf.

Boris, E. T. & Maronick, M. (2012). Civic Participation and Advocacy. In L. M. Salamon, ed. *The State of Nonprofit America*, 2nd ed. Washington, DC: Brookings Institution Press, pp. 394–422.

Brody, B. (2018). Business Groups Spent Big on Lobbying during the Tax Overhaul. *Bloomberg News*, January 23. www.bloomberg.com/news/articles/2018-01-23/tax-bill-prompts-business-to-pay-heavily-for-lobbying-campaigns#xj4y7vzkg.

Cary, P. & Holmes, A. (2019). The Secret Saga of Trump's Tax Cuts. Center for Public Integrity, April 30. https://publicintegrity.org/inequality-poverty-opportunity/taxes/trumps-tax-cuts/the-secret-saga-of-trumps-tax-cuts/.

Coble, R. (1999). The Nonprofit Sector and State Governments: Public Policy Issues Facing Nonprofits in North Carolina and Other States. *Nonprofit Management & Leadership*. 9(1), 293–313. https://onlinelibrary.wiley.com/doi/abs/10.1002/nml.9306.

Council on Foundations (no date). History of the Council on Foundations. https://cof.org/sites/default/files/documents/files/History%20of%20the%20Council%20on%20Foundations.pdf.

Council on Foundations (1980). Principles and Practices for Effective Grantmaking. Reprinted in *The Philanthropist Journal*. https://thephilanthropist.ca/original-pdfs/Philanthropist-3-1-547.pdf.

Crandall-Hollick, M. I. (2020). The Charitable Deduction for Individuals: A Brief Legislative History. Congressional Research Service, June 26. https://crsreports.congress.gov/product/pdf/R/R46178/3.

Daniels, A. (2017). Charities Are Divided Over Efforts to Kill the Estate Tax. *Chronicle of Philanthropy*, October 30. www.philanthropy.com/article/charities-are-divided-over-efforts-to-kill-the-estate-tax/.

Daniels, A. (2019). Nonprofits and Foundations Poised to Score Victories in Tax Legislation. *Chronicle of Philanthropy*, December 17. www.philanthropy.com/article/nonprofits-and-foundations-poised-to-score-victories-in-tax-legislation/.

Daniels, A. (2020). Wealthy Donors to Congress: Make Us Give More to Charity. *Chronicle of Philanthropy*, May 13. www.philanthropy.com/article/wealthy-donors-to-congress-make-us-give-more-to-charity/?cid2=gen_login_refresh&cid=gen_sign_in.

Daniels, A. & O'Neil, M. (2017a). Giving Could Plunge $13 Billion under Tax Plan, Nonprofit Leader Says. *Chronicle of Philanthropy*, September 27. www.philanthropy.com/article/giving-could-plunge-13-billion-under-tax-plan-nonprofit-leader-says/.

Daniels, A. & O'Neil, M. (2017b). Nonprofit Leaders Urge Pence to Expand Charitable Donation. *Chronicle of Philanthropy*, July 13. www.philanthropy.com/article/nonprofit-leaders-urge-pence-to-expand-charitable-deduction/?cid2=gen_login_refresh&cid=gen_sign_in.

Daniels, A. & Theis, M. (2020). Nonprofits Coming up Short So Far in Congressional Stimulus Negotiations. *Chronicle of Philanthropy*, December 16. www.philanthropy.com/article/nonprofits-come-up-short-in-congressional-stimulus-negotiations.

Davis, J. H. & Rappaport, A. (2017). Trump Proposes the Most Sweeping Tax Overhaul in Decades. *New York Times* September 27. www.nytimes.com/2017/09/27/us/politics/trump-tax-cut-plan-middle-class-deficit.html.

DeBonis, M. & Werner, E. (2017). How Republicans Pulled Off the Biggest Tax Overhaul in 30 Years. *Washington Post*, December 20. www.washingtonpost.com/business/economy/how-the-republicans-pulled-off-the-biggest-tax-overhaul-in-30-years/2017/12/20/efcba3c4-e54e-11e7-ab50-621fe0588340_story.html.

Dennis, K. A. (no date). Note from Philanthropy Magazine's First Editor. Philanthropy Roundtable. www.philanthropyroundtable.org/magazine/a-note-from-philanthropy-magazines-first-editor/.

Dias, E. (2017). President Trump Lost a Fight to Allow Churches to Get More Involved in Politics. *Time*, December 15. https://time.com/5067035/president-trump-lost-a-fight-to-allow-churches-to-get-more-involved-in-politics/.

Duquette, N. J. (2019). Founders' Fortunes and Philanthropy: A History of the U.S. Charitable-Contribution Deduction. *Business History Review* 93 (Autumn): 553–584. https://doi.org/10.1017/S0007680519000710.

Eastman, S. (2019). How Many Taxpayers Itemize under Current Law. *Tax Foundation*, September 12. https://taxfoundation.org/standard-deduction-itemized-deductions-current-law-2019/#:~:text=We%20estimate%20about%2013.7%20percent,40%20percent%20to%2060%20percent).

Edelman (Various years). Edelman Trust Barometer. www.edelman.com/trust/trust-barometer.

Frumkin, P. (1998). The Long Recoil from Regulation: Private Philanthropic Foundations and the Tax Reform Act of 1969. *American Review of Public Administration* 28(3): 266–286. https://journals.sagepub.com/doi/pdf/10.1177/027507409802800303.

Gale, W., Gelfond, H., Krupkin, A., Mazur, M. J., & Toder, E. (2018). A Preliminary Assessment of the Tax Cuts and Jobs Act of 2017. *National Tax Journal* 71(4): 589–611. www.journals.uchicago.edu/doi/epdf/10.17310/ntj.2018.4.01.

Giving USA Foundation (2019). *Giving USA 2019: The Annual Report on Philanthropy for the Year 2018*. Researched and Written by the Indiana University Lilly Family School of Philanthropy. www.givingusa.org.

Goldfeder, M. A. & Terry, M. K. (2017). To Repeal or Not Repeal: The Johnson Amendment. *University of Memphis Law Review* 48(1): 209–255. https://acrobat.adobe.com/id/urn:aaid:sc:US:943f0c07-d731-48ef-8694-b71b9c78bf61.

Hall, P. D. (1992). *Inventing the Nonprofit Sector and Other Essays on Philanthropy, Voluntarism, and Nonprofit Organizations*. Baltimore, MD: Johns Hopkins University Press.

Haynes, E. (2020). California's New Privacy Law Draws Attention from Nonprofits. *Chronicle of Philanthropy*, January 1. www.philanthropy.com/article/californias-new-privacy-law-draws-attention-from-nonprofits/.

Independent Sector (2021). Trust in Civil Society. https://independentsector.org/resource/trust-in-civil-society-2021/.

References

Internal Revenue Service (2021). Tax on Unrelated Business Income of Exempt Organizations. Publication 598. www.irs.gov/pub/irs-pdf/p598.pdf.

Johnson, C. (2017). The GOP Plan to Simplify Taxes Could Put Charitable Giving at Risk. *Washington Post*, October 11. www.washingtonpost.com/news/wonk/wp/2017/10/11/the-gop-plan-to-simplify-taxes-could-put-charitable-giving-at-risk/.

Kenyon, D. A. & A. H. Langley (2010). Payments in Lieu of Taxes: Balancing Municipal and Nonprofit Interests. Cambridge, MA: Lincoln Institute of Land Policy. www.lincolninst.edu/sites/default/files/pubfiles/payments-in-lieu-of-taxes-full_0.pdf.

Knoll, M. S. (2007). The UBIT: Leveling an Uneven Playing Field or Tilting a Level One? *Fordham Law Review* 76(2): 857–892. https://ir.lawnet.fordham.edu/cgi/viewcontent.cgi?article=4314&context=flr.

Koenig, R. (2016). Independent Sector Lays Off One-Quarter of Its Staff. *Chronicle of Philanthropy*, December 8. www.philanthropy.com/article/independent-sector-lays-off-one-quarter-of-its-staff/.

Long, H. (2017). In Small Win for Democrats, the Final Tax Bill Will Not Include a Provision Allowing Churches to Endorse Political Candidates. *Washington Post*, December 14. www.washingtonpost.com/news/wonk/wp/2017/12/14/in-small-win-for-democrats-the-final-tax-bill-wont-include-a-provision-to-allow-churches-to-endorse-political-candidates/.

Lott, C. M., Shelly, M. L., Dietz, N., & Mitchell, G. E. (2023). The Regulatory Breadth Index: A New Tool for the Measurement and Comparison of State-Level Charity Regulation in the United States. *Nonprofit Management and Leadership* 33(3): 633–645. https://doi.org/10.1002/nml.21536.

Lott, C. M., Shelly, M., Kunstler Goldman, K., et al. (2019). Legal Compendium. *Urban Institute*, October 29. www.urban.org/sites/default/files/2019/12/06/legal_compendium_oct_2019_update_.xlsx.

McDonald, E. K. (2021). Let Them Give: Philanthropic Infrastructure and Industry in the United States. PhD dissertation. Department of Sociology, George Mason University, Fairfax, VA.

McKeever, B. S., Dietz, N., & Fyffe, S. (2016). *The Nonprofit Almanac: The Essential Facts and Figures for Managers, Researchers, and Volunteers*. Lanham, MD: Rowman and Littlefield, co-published with the Urban Institute Press.

Mitchell, G. E. (2023). Three Models of US State-Level Charity Regulation. *Nonprofit Policy Forum*. https://doi.org/10.1515/npf-2022-0051.

National Council of Nonprofits (2019). Nonprofit Impact Matters: How America's Charitable Nonprofits Strengthen Communities and Improve

Lives. www.nonprofitimpactmatters.org/site/assets/files/1/nonprofit-impact-matters-sept-2019-1.pdf.

Nonprofit Times (2017). Johnson Amendment Saved for Now. December 15. www.thenonprofittimes.com/npt_articles/johnson-amendment-saved-now/#.

O'Connell, B. (1997). *Powered by Coalition: The Story of INDEPENDENT SECTOR.* San Francisco, CA: Jossey-Bass.

Parks, D. (2020). Some Nonprofits Hail Paycheck Protection Program as a "Savior"; Others See Layoffs Continue. *Chronicle of Philanthropy*, July 21. www.philanthropy.com/article/some-nonprofits-hail-paycheck-protection-program-as-a-savior-others-see-layoffs-continue.

Parks, D. & Theis, M. (2020). Nonprofits Win Extended Charitable Deduction and Paycheck Protection Loans in Stimulus Bill. *Chronicle of Philanthropy*, December 21. www.philanthropy.com/article/nonprofits-win-extended-charitable-deductions-and-paycheck-protection-loans-in-stimulus-bill.

Penna, R. M. (2018). The Johnson Amendment: Fact-checking the Narrative. *Stanford Social Innovation Review*, August 24. https://ssir.org/articles/entry/the_johnson_amendment_fact_checking_the_narrative.

Perry, S. (2009a). Foundation Group Opposes Charitable-Deduction Cap and Supports Estate Tax. *Chronicle of Philanthropy*, March 11. www.philanthropy.com/article/foundation-group-opposes-charitable-deduction-cap-and-supports-estate-tax/.

Perry, S. (2009b). Independent Sector Says Obama Deduction Plan Presents "Solomon's Choice." *Chronicle of Philanthropy*, March 27. www.philanthropy.com/article/independent-sector-says-obama-deduction-plan-presents-solomons-choice/.

Perry, S. (2009c). Nonprofit Groups Urge Taxing the Wealthy to Help Finance Health Plan. *Chronicle of Philanthropy*, July 9. www.philanthropy.com/article/nonprofit-groups-urge-taxing-the-wealthy-to-help-finance-health-plan/.

Perry, S. (2009d). Obama Defends Proposal to Limit Charity Breaks for the Wealthy. *Chronicle of Philanthropy*, April 9. www.philanthropy.com/article/obama-defends-proposal-to-limit-charity-breaks-for-the-wealthy/.

Perry, S. & Preston, C. (2009). A Taxing Proposition. *Chronicle of Philanthropy*, March 12. www.philanthropy.com/article/a-taxing-proposition/.

Philanthropy Daily (2021). Conservative Author and Venture Capitalist J. D. Vance: Eliminate All Special Tax Privileges for Foundations, May 20. https://philanthropydaily.com/conservative-author-and-venture-capitalist-j-d-vance-eliminate-all-special-tax-privileges-for-foundations/.

Reid, E. J. (1999). Nonprofit Advocacy and Political Participation. In E. T. Boris & C. E. Steuerle, eds. *Nonprofits and Government:*

Collaboration and Conflict. 1st ed. Washington, DC: Urban Institute, pp. 291–325.

Salamon, L. M. & Newhouse, C. L. (2020). The 2020 Nonprofit Employment Report. Nonprofit Economic Data Bulletin No. 48. Baltimore, MD: Johns Hopkins University Center for Civil Society Studies. https://baypath.s3.amazonaws.com/files/resources/2020-nonprofit-employment-report-final-6-2020.pdf.

Schadler, B. H. (2022). The Connection: Strategies for Creating and Operating 501(c)(3)s, 501(c)(4)s and Political Organizations. 4th ed. Washington, DC: Alliance for Justice. https://afj.org/wp-content/uploads/2022/01/AFJ_CONNECTION_RPT_2022-1.pdf.

Sherlock, M. F. & Gravelle, J. G. (2009). An Overview of the Nonprofit and Charitable Sector. Congressional Research Service. https://crsreports.congress.gov/product/pdf/R/R40919/3.

Suarez, D. (2020). Advocacy, Civic Engagement, and Social Change. In W. W. Powell & P. Bromley, eds. *The Nonprofit Sector: A Research Handbook*. 3rd ed. Stanford, CA: Stanford University Press, pp. 491–506.

Swan, J. (2017). Republicans Agree to Raise Bottom Tax Rate, Double Standard Deduction. *Axios*, September 26. www.axios.com/2017/12/15/republicans-agree-to-raise-bottom-tax-rate-double-standard-deduction-1513305776.

Theis, M. (2020). Small Nonprofits Struggle to Get Payroll Loans in New Federal Program. *Chronicle of Philanthropy*, April 6. www.philanthropy.com/article/small-nonprofits-struggle-to-get-payroll-loans-in-new-federal-program/.

Tocqueville, A. D. (1969). *Democracy in America*. Translated by G. Lawrence, edited by J. P. Mayer. Garden City, NY: Anchor Books, Doubleday.

Vogel, K. P. & Goodstein, L. (2017). In Tax Debate, Gift to Religious Right Could Be Bargaining Chip. *New York Times*, November 26. www.nytimes.com/2017/11/26/us/politics/johnson-amendment-churches-taxes-politics.html.

Vogel, K. P. & Tankersley, J. (2017). With Billions at Stake in Tax Debate, Lobbyists Play Hardball. *New York Times*, December 15. www.nytimes.com/2017/12/15/us/politics/lobbyists-tax-overhaul-congress.html.

Williams, A. I. & Doan, D. R. H. (2021). Independent Sector: Preserving the Status Quo. *Nonprofit Policy Forum* 12(2): 341–366. https://doi.org/10.1515/npf-2020-0014.

Wolverton, B. (2004). Senators Ask for Suggestions to Shape Nonprofit Legislation. *Chronicle of Philanthropy*, October 14. www.philanthropy.com/article/senators-ask-for-suggestions-to-shape-nonprofit-legislation/.

Wong, A. & Fattal, I. (2017). The Tax Bill Provision That Would Cost Harvard Millions. *The Atlantic*, November 30. www.theatlantic.com/education/archive/2017/11/the-tax-bill-provision-that-would-cost-harvard-millions/547175/.

Young, D. R. (1999). Complementary, Supplementary, or Adversarial? A Theoretical and Historical Examination of Nonprofit-Government Relations in the United States. In E. T. Boris & C. E. Steuerle, eds. *Nonprofits and Government: Collaboration and Conflict*. 1st ed. Washington, DC: Urban Institute, pp. 31–67.

Acknowledgements

The authors are grateful to many individuals who informed and supported their work. Our many interviewees gave generously of their time to enlighten us about key events and processes, including several who were interviewed more than once. Multiple research assistants at George Mason University – including Kat Krupenevich, Mike Sweeney, Mike Sweigart, and especially Emily Rogers – helped greatly with background research for this project. The authors appreciate the early encouragement of Jeff Berry, thoughtful suggestions from anonymous reviewers, and the support of the series editors, Andy Whitford and Rob Christensen. Victoria Vrana and her colleagues at the Bill and Melinda Gates provided funding and encouragement for this study and enabled the open access availability of this Element. The ASAE Foundation also awarded grant support for this project. Finally, Alan Abramson appreciates the continuing encouragement of his husband, Alex, who will check for his name in these acknowledgments even if he does not read any of the text; Benjamin Soskis dedicates this book to the memory of his father, David Aaron Soskis, who passed away while it was being prepared.

Cambridge Elements

Public and Nonprofit Administration

Andrew Whitford
University of Georgia

Andrew Whitford is Alexander M. Crenshaw Professor of Public Policy in the School of Public and International Affairs at the University of Georgia. His research centers on strategy and innovation in public policy and organization studies.

Robert Christensen
Brigham Young University

Robert Christensen is professor and George Romney Research Fellow in the Marriott School at Brigham Young University. His research focuses on prosocial and antisocial behaviors and attitudes in public and nonprofit organizations.

About the Series

The foundation of this series are cutting-edge contributions on emerging topics and definitive reviews of keystone topics in public and nonprofit administration, especially those that lack longer treatment in textbook or other formats. Among keystone topics of interest for scholars and practitioners of public and nonprofit administration, it covers public management, public budgeting and finance, nonprofit studies, and the interstitial space between the public and nonprofit sectors, along with theoretical and methodological contributions, including quantitative, qualitative and mixed-methods pieces.

The Public Management Research Association

The Public Management Research Association improves public governance by advancing research on public organizations, strengthening links among interdisciplinary scholars, and furthering professional and academic opportunities in public management.

PMRA
public management research association

Cambridge Elements

Public and Nonprofit Administration

Elements in the Series

Contingent Collaboration: When to Use Which Models for Joined-up Government
Rodney J. Scott and Eleanor R. K. Merton

The Hidden Tier of Social Services: Frontline Workers' Provision of Informal Resources in the Public, Nonprofit, and Private Sectors
Einat Lavee

Networks in the Public Sector: A Multilevel Framework and Systematic Review
Michael D. Siciliano, Weijie Wang, Qian Hu, Alejandra Medina, and David Krackhardt

Organizing and Institutionalizing Local Sustainability: A Design Approach
Aaron Deslatte

When Governments Lobby Governments: The Institutional Origins of Intergovernmental Persuasion in America
Youlang Zhang

Public Administration and Democracy: The Complementarity Principle
Anthony M. Bertelli and Lindsey J. Schwartz

Redefining Development: Resolving Complex Challenges in a Global Context 2nd edition
Jessica Kritz

Experts in Government: The Deep State from Caligula to Trump and Beyond
Donald F. Kettl

New Public Governance as a Hybrid: A Critical Interpretation
Laura Cataldi

Can Governance be Intelligent?: An Interdisciplinary Approach and Evolutionary Modelling for Intelligent Governance in the Digital Age
Eran Vigoda-Gadot

The Courts and the President: Judicial Review of Presidentially Directed Action
Charles Wise

Standing Up for Nonprofits: Advocacy on Federal, Sector-wide Issues
Alan J. Abramson and Benjamin Soskis

A full series listing is available at: www.cambridge.org/EPNP

Milton Keynes UK
Ingram Content Group UK Ltd.
UKHW020121070624
443692UK00005B/162